Usain Bolt

Usain Bolt

The story of the
world's fastest man

STEVEN DOWNES

SPORTS
BOOKS

Published by SportsBooks Ltd
November 2011

Copyright: Steven Downes 2011

SportsBooks Limited
1 Evelyn Court
Malvern Road
Cheltenham
GL50 2JR
United Kingdom
Tel: 01242 256755
Fax: 0560 3108126
e-mail   info@sportsbooks.ltd.uk
Website   www.sportsbooks.ltd.uk

Cover designed by Alan Hunns

Cover photograph of Usain Bolt by Mark Shearman

Statistics on Usain Bolt's career provided by Mirko Javala and on world record progression by Peter Matthews

A CIP catalogue record for this book is available from the British Library.

ISBN 978-1-907524-18-9

Printed and bound by CPI Group (UK) Ltd, Croydon, CR0 4YY

Contents

	Acknowledgements	vii
	The Warm Up	1
Chapter 1	On Your Marks	9
Chapter 2	Get Set	29
Chapter 3	Go!	47
Chapter 4	How Does He Do It?	64
Chapter 5	Bolt, his BMW and Berlin	81
Chapter 6	False Start	112
Chapter 7	Redemption Song	145
	Statistics	
	Usain Bolt's career	158
	World record progression	163
	Olympic champions	166
	World champions	168
	About the author	170

Acknowledgements

THEY SAY THAT athletics books don't sell. I've never yet managed to pin down exactly who 'they' are, but over the course of the past few months, I have managed to determine someone who is very much not one of them.

That's Randall Northam, the owner of SportsBooks Ltd and the publisher of this volume, and a rare beast in these days of Amazon, Kindles, t'interweb and the 30-second attention span.

Randall and I have known one another for many years. It is more than twenty since we jousted weekly over a hundred pages or more of athletics news, features and results, he as the editor of *Athletics Today*, me clinging on for dear life at the helm of *Athletics Weekly*.

Randall has spent the last dozen years or so cultivating a splendid niche in the publishing world, often taking on books that other publishers had declined as not being commercial enough. His books are usually written by experts or enthusiasts, people who really know their stuff, and they are always fascinatingly interesting.

So modesty demands that I ought to question why he has taken on this book.

But then you really do have to question why he would not. Even in this television-dominated age, there's a healthy market in cricket books, and some in golf, too. Football books about 'how I spent 25 years suffering as a fan of Man United/Arsenal/Man City' seem to roll out of the printers on a weekly basis.

But books about track and field? All too few and far between, even when one of the world's top five sports stars happens to be a sprinter.

So thank you, Randall, for giving me the opportunity and also having the patience to deal with my authorial shortcomings.

I should also like to thank Norman Giller, who has recently become an old mate, and provides constant inspiration about the business of sports writing.

Thanks, too, to Patrick Collins, of the *Mail on Sunday*, Paul Kimmage, in the *Sunday Times*, and Martin Kelner, in the *Guardian*, for weekly demonstrating how it ought to be done.

The BBC, for all its faults, deserves recognition for its generally reliable coverage of international athletics, on TV, on radio (Mike Costello is an under-rated diamond of a commentator and expert, both on the track and in the ring), and online. The BBC documentary by Michael Johnson about Bolt earlier this year was a fascinating watch, and provided much more insight and background to life in Trelawny.

The IAAF, specifically Nick Davies and Chris Turner, also deserve thanks because, through their patience and tolerance, I have had the privilege and (some) pleasure of attending so many of the world governing body's events over the past three decades, often as a member of their reporting team.

If anyone, apart from U St L Bolt himself, is responsible for 'inspiring' this book, it is the aforesaid Davies, a one-time training partner of Linford Christie no less, who has spent the past twenty years based in Monte Carlo. Poor lamb.

But it was Nick who inflicted upon me a week in Sherbrooke and so gave me my first encounter with Bolt. Truly, it was a moment which has stayed with me ever since.

We have made attributions to newspapers, magazines and books wherever possible. I can recommend Bolt's own ghosted biography, *9.58*, provided it is read with that fistful of salt that acknowledges that it offers only a view via the carefully honed prism through which the sprinter – or, more probably, his management and 'handlers' – would prefer you to see him.

That book is also, perforce, already dated. Writing a book about a moving target, especially one that moves as fast as Bolt, is inevitably only going to provide a snapshot of history, and from one point of view.

And it is from my point of view that this book also owes a vote of thanks to Jennifer Bolt, Wellesley Bolt, and yes, Usain Bolt. It's been a pleasure and a privilege to follow your career, thus far.

There's a bottle of Guinness in it for you, in the Hole in the Wall in Waterloo, when you visit London next August.

Steven Downes
London, November 2011

The Warm Up

bolt[1] *n.* Short heavy arrow of crossbow; discharge of lightning (~ from the blue, complete surprise); door-fastening of sliding bar and staple; metal pin with head for holding things together, usu. riveted or with nut.

bolt[2] *v.* **1.** *v.i. & t.* Dart off or away, (of horse) escape from control; run to seed; (cause fox, rabbit etc. to) escape from hole or burrow; gulp down hastily without chewing; ~ **hole** (fig.) means of escape. **2.** *v. t.* Fasten (door etc.) with bolt. Keep in or out with bolting door.

bolt[3] *n.* Act of bolting; sudden start; running away.

HIS VERY NAME suggests speed, and in so many ways.

A simple four-letter word which in the English language is widely understood to imply rapidity. A sudden start? Well that will be part of this story. A means of escape? Well that, too, in some respects. 'With head for holding things together', to take the liberty of abbreviating one definition, will provide us with another element of this account.

When Usain St Leo Bolt hove into the view of the global media in early 2008, the headline writers' union ought to have had a whip-round. And a generous one, at that. It was Olympic year, and here was a promising new star in their firmament, possibly the biggest star, and he would look after all their back-page leads, and some on the front pages, too, for the coming summer and well beyond. The fastest man the world has ever seen could not have chosen a better, more fitting name, had he done so by deed poll.

And yet, nearly four years later, do the billions of people who have watched, and enjoyed, Bolt's record-breaking exploits, whether on television or, if they have been really fortunate, in person, really know much more about the man now, in his twenty-fifth year and approaching his third Olympic Games, than they did when the gawky teenager turned up in Athens in 2004 and departed almost unnoticed after failing to get beyond the heats of his event?

For there are other definitions of the word 'bolt' which are also apposite. 'Keep in or out with bolting door'; 'escape from hole or burrow'.

The paradox is intense. Here you have one of the world's hottest commercial sporting properties, whose public appearances and utterances outside the track have become as scarce as raindrops in the Sahara.

In 2009 Bolt was in Berlin, the city where seven decades earlier, Adolf Hitler had strutted his Aryan domination stuff all over the pliant Lords of the Olympic Rings. History records that in 1936, Jesse Owens, with four gold medals in his knapsack by the end of those jackbooted Games, was the ultimate winner in that little sporting stand-off.

Bolt may have managed to win 'only' three gold medals at the 2009 World Championships (unlike Owens, Bolt does not try the long jump, probably because his dodgy back would not allow him to), but when it came to winning over the German public, the 21st-century sprinter was light-years ahead. The hottest clothing items for blond-haired and blue-eyed German kids were Puma-branded T-shirts in the joyful colours of Jamaica, carrying an image of Bolt in his 'trademark' (and possibly trademarked) lightning bolt pose. The Berlin Wall may have come down two decades earlier, but now Bolt was breaking down any further lingering barriers between the races in Germany.

Two years later, the eager anticipation of Bolt's Olympic 100 metres defence in London in August 2012 saw more than one million people apply for tickets to see the final of that event alone. The London organisers could have sold out their stadium twelve times over, all for a race unlikely to last more than ten seconds, with some punters willing to pay more than £2,000 for the privilege of being able to tell their grandchildren 'I was there' – and those prices were before any tickets found their way on to the black market.

By mid-2011, Usain Bolt, one of the world's most recognisable sports stars, had given no one-on-one interviews to newspapers or magazines, never mind to mere book writers, for two years. Outside the televised confines of the world's biggest athletics stadiums, the man who in 2009 had covered 100 metres of the cobalt blue Berlin track in just 9.58 seconds had somehow become remarkably slow when it came to coming forward to talk about himself, his training, his congenital back condition, his views and ambitions.

Perhaps that rarity value of Bolt is working for his agents and sponsors, as the little that the public gets to see or hear of the world's greatest ever sprinter – because that is what he most certainly is – creates an ever-more hysterical appetite for his mugging to the TV cameras before race starts and his disjointed dance efforts after his latest victory. The rumoured fee of $100,000 per race – even a sub-10-second 100 metres one – is the premium rate route to sprinting away from any global recession.

There is little doubt, though, that Bolt's handlers are plotting a careful game around their charge. When in 2009 Bolt signed a mega-publishing deal with a Rupert Murdoch-owned subsidiary to tell his own life story, the ghostwriter hired was not a specialist Olympics or athletics journalist, but a football reporter from the tabloid *Sun* newspaper who had never before in person even seen his subject run.

When, at a press conference ahead of the annual Paris Grand Prix meeting in 2010 Bolt was asked whether his account of his own life would reveal very much, he said, 'You can't really give away anything in your book ... Should be exciting, it's my life, and I'm a cool and exciting guy.' That's hardly the sort of 'sales spiel' to make publishers rich.

Thus, ahead of the London Olympics, the Jamaican has become more of an enigma to the wider public than he was in the summers of 2008 and 2009, when we all first witnessed how with just a few of his powerful, gigantic strides, Usain Bolt seemed able to turn the very world itself.

It is quite certain, too, that Bolt the enigma will continue to create endless fascination.

Even Maurice Greene, the 'Kansas Cannonball' to give him his quaint, slightly old world, prizefighter-style nickname, had never seen anything like it.

Greene was at a reception hosted by one of the world's two biggest sporting goods manufacturers, a company that had effectively been paying him a six-figure salary for the past decade.

In the large, bright hotel reception room, over chilled fruit juices and canapés, the former world and Olympic champion was fielding questions from the press about a phenomenon that seemed certain to alter his sporting world beyond recognition. After all, if we could not get access to The Man himself (who we were reliably informed at the time was on some kind of 24-hour bender, celebrating the conjunction of his latest man speed record and his birthday), then we were going to make sure that we got at least a line or two from someone who, not so long before, had been placed on an equally high and precarious pedestal.

Greene looked at his questioner, and posed a question himself.

'Usain Bolt?' asked the American, himself once the holder of the world record for the 100 metres dash and, therefore, 'the world's fastest man', probably the most desired sporting title on the planet.

'Don't you mean Insane Bolt?' Greene said, laughing enthusiastically at his own joke, clearly of the mind that the world of sport was going slightly, well... mad.

It was another morning after the night before; less hung-over, though, more just shell-shocked. Anyone connected with track and field athletics was in Berlin for the World Championships being staged there, and still breathless, rendered almost speechless by what they had witnessed in the Olympiastadion the previous evening.

In less than 12 months, Usain Bolt had transformed his event, his sport, and the world of sport, bursting on to the global stage like a green and gold meteor. Only, possibly, just a little bit faster.

By that week of his twenty-third birthday, the young Jamaican had claimed his fifth and sixth world records, and added three world championship titles to the three Olympic gold medals he had won in such breathtaking manner in Beijing's Birdnest Stadium the year before.

And now, comparisons in all-time sporting greatness were being made between Owens and Bolt. For unlike so many other, modern track sprinters, who snarled and growled their way to sub-10-second performances, apparently contemptuous of their rivals and the fans, Bolt was transforming his sport with a smile, that pose and even a dance.

Every night that Bolt was due to race in Berlin, the stadium would fill with 80,000 people eager to catch an all-too-brief glimpse of this legend in the making.

The sport's top officials were caught up in an almost unseemly haste to present Bolt with his world record bonus cheque, to hang his medal around his neck, or to be at the next photo opportunity. Bolt's shoe sponsors rushed out – at eighty euro per pair – flat-soled replicas of Bolt's Mambo spiked racing shoes.

Track and field athletics, for so long joyless and beleaguered after a series of disfiguring doping scandals, suddenly had a smile back on its face, a smile placed there by one man. Usain Bolt. This is the story of Bolt's life and very fast times.

Chapter 1

On Your Marks

THANKFULLY BY EARLY evening, the heavy showers that had managed to drench the competitors and officials during the morning session, as well as thousands of spectators in uncovered seats in the new stadium, had abated. Now, a 'second shift' of sports fans was beginning to arrive at Stratford's two rail stations, to be squeezed out of the Tubes and trains to make the short walk into the Olympic Park.

Many of these are the people with the hottest ticket of the year, possibly the decade. There's a family there. Four of them: mum, dad and two kids, a boy about eight years old perhaps, holding tightly on to his mother's hand so as not to get lost in the crush of people, while his sister, probably two years or so older, is being led equally carefully by her father.

It was more than a year ago that the family decided to enter an online ballot for tickets. Although they live in south London, not too far from Crystal Palace, where record-breaking televised track meetings had been staged for the previous forty years, they had never been to an athletics event before. The children had been too young, getting back from work on a

Friday had never been easy, and besides, you could never get tickets for the bigger meets, they were always sold out months in advance.

But when they saw that the Olympics were coming to London, the father checked the schedule because they had all heard of one runner and thought that this would be a great chance to see him race. When they had seen this runner on television the previous summer, the little boy had copied the victory pose and used it around the house for days afterwards.

So his father dutifully went to the Olympics website – he was doing this for his children, of course, and not for himself at all. He ticked a couple of boxes, filled in his details and then sat back and waited.

About six weeks later, when nearly £1,200 was added on to his credit card bill (he went back to double check he had not ordered twenty tickets by mistake), he realised that they had got what he had ordered. He allowed himself a quiet, inner sigh that he had not ticked the box for the most expensive seats, and reminded himself not to mention the full cost to his wife.

And so now, more than a year later, here they all were for their once-in-a-lifetime experience. They had taken a train through the suburbs to London Bridge station, which seemed much busier than on a regular summer Sunday, and where the London 2012 banners and colours were noticeably on display, draped from lamp posts and the metal beams beneath the towering glistening Shard, London's new tallest building. There, they dived down below ground by escalator to change on to the Jubilee Line – they were never going to risk London's traffic by trying to drive to Stratford. Besides, where could they have parked?

Even in the week beforehand, when he had stayed up well past his usual bedtime to watch the Olympic flame being lit, the eight-year-old had been getting increasingly excited. He had practised his pose more than once. On the Tube, he would jab his finger in the direction of other passengers, those he spotted possibly with the same destination, reading their official Olympic programmes, or copies of *Athletics Weekly*.

The whole journey took a little less than an hour, so once the family got to Stratford, they still had some time before the stadium gates opened. They followed the crowd, a great mass of people, a cross-section of Londoners, Britons and visitors from abroad, some wrapped in their national flag. More than one or two had the colours of Jamaica around their shoulders.

There is little doubt that any gathering together such as this of a large group of humanity, for a sports event, for a concert, maybe a religious festival, can have a discernible effect on the people, and transform the arena that contains them. The late Geoffrey Green, the revered one-time 'Association football correspondent' for *The Times*, felt that on match days the arrival of the tens of thousands of people would bring life to the stadium.

'During the week the curved wall of the arena, any arena, is still and lonely, a big cement circle surrounding emptiness with only the wind to rattle its hoardings. But on Saturday afternoons during the season the curve of that wall comes to life. It reaches out in a big sweep like a magnet and draws into itself something vibrant, full of warmth and powerful feeling.'

Go to any sports stadium when it is closed and empty, and all you have is a building. Arrive at a stadium even hours before the competition begins on the day of a big event, and the energy almost sparks from the pavement.

It is as if the presence of the spectators is in some way fused with the building around them, animating the stadium. 'The arena, that sunlit, or shaded, or wet stage for a drama no one can foretell, is touched of a sudden with a magic colour and hum from that crowd,' Green wrote. 'You are ready to forfeit yourself for a short span to the heart of the battle.'

And so it is with our family, as they join the crowd snaking towards the Olympic Park, there to see the 'drama no one can foretell'. Each individual member of the crowd, no doubt, has the final page of their own script already clear in their own mind. Yet by the end of the evening, each one will have a hi-res video of what they have all witnessed, from 80,000 different individual angles, all hard-wired into their personal hard drive's memory, never to be erased.

JB Priestley, in his novel *The Good Companions*, described a crowd of sports fans in the north of England, few of whom might still be alive by 2012. Yet their characteristics as a group are being replicated here, in the 21st century, hundreds of miles away in Europe's newest and biggest urban park: '...the road itself cannot be seen at all. A grey-green tide flows sluggishly down its length...' Priestley wrote more than eighty years before.

'To say that these men' – they were all men in Priestley's day, and the prices and the currency were different then, too, 'paid their shillings to watch twenty-two hirelings kick a ball is merely to say that a violin is wood and cat-gut, that Hamlet is so much paper and ink.'

And in today's drama, there would be no play without its prince.

Many of the world's major sports stadiums – Berlin, Beijing's Bird's Nest, the Camp Nou in Barcelona, the Melbourne Cricket Ground, even Wembley, old and new – have maintained their 'wow factor' years after their construction. Even today, as you walk towards the Colosseum in Rome, the sense of awe at its structural magnificence, some two thousand years after it was built, leads you to think that even one of the greatest of modern movie directors, Ridley Scott, failed to capture the real scale of Rome in his *Gladiator*.

Often it is just the sheer scale of the building, all blended in together with a hefty dose of anticipation of what you are about to witness, that can set aflutter butterflies in the stomach of even the most cynical and experienced of old hacks.

For the tens of thousands of spectators streaming from the rail stations, through the shopping mall and into London's Olympic Park on this slightly steamy summer's evening, that sense of shock and awe when they first see the stadium is somehow missing. First, they have had to negotiate the security checks at the entrance to the park.

The mother of our little family can be overheard, more than once, trying to placate her impatient son, who seems primed to set off on a sprint of his own, given half a chance. 'This is why we got here so early,' she says to the child. 'The queues will be a lot longer later on, and you want to have the chance to have a good look round, don't you?' Her daughter smiles, wanly, at her brother and tries again to read the programme her father has just reluctantly paid £10 for and handed over in another gesture of sacrifice.

Once past the X-ray machines and bag checks, some of the spectators peel off and head towards the Aquatics Centre, where a final is about to get under way in the diving events. Even this building, with its roof arching in the shape of a swimming ray fish, does not quite take the casual passer-by's breath away. With the extra few thousand temporary seats, all in a box that looks almost bolted on to the side of the building for the duration of the Games, the symmetry of the architect's lofty yet impractical design is wrecked.

The bulk of the group, the athletics crowd, presses on determinedly, a broad bridge over a cleaned-up tributary of the River Thames, to cross before stepping into the shadow of their destination. Yet even now, the only thing that is setting the heart rate apace is the sense of hurry through the horde, the desire not to miss anything.

It might be because London's stadium is partially 'buried' below ground level, the bottom-most tier of seats having been dug deep into the ground. From outside, the stadium appears barely two-thirds its full height.

Even so, it is also not the biggest stadium you might ever encounter, with a capacity of 80,000, rather than the near 100,000 spectators who were able to get into Sydney's Olympic Stadium in 2000 or in Beijing four years ago. It was in Beijing, after all, where it all really started, where a legend was created. But that was then...

London's new stadium has a temporary feel about it, too. After all, 'temporary' was the architects' original brief, because no one in a position of authority at the Games organisers, or those in charge of what claims to be the Greatest City in the World, had the confidence to justify having a large multi-sport stadium after the 2012 Olympic circus had packed up its tents and moved on to its next host city.

The temporary nature of the venue is emphasised by the surrounding large white steel tubes, just like scaffolding, criss-crossing the outside of the arena, forming a massive, spiky crown around the rim of the stadium. The massive coloured plastic 'wrap' that forms the skin around the stadium reinforces the transient look, making it appear to be contained within a cheap supermarket carrier bag.

And the boy can now see the other, almost temporary structure alongside the stadium, 'Look, mummy, look!' he implores, pointing again, this time at the tall hulk of rusty-red steel that appears to be a memorial to thousands of half-eaten Curly-Wurlies.

Past another concessions stand, selling burgers or sweet fizzy drinks, or 2012 memorabilia, keyrings, cutlery sets, or more versions of the official mascots, the one-eyed embodiments of a CCTV camera, unwittingly characterising the modern London so well.

Our spectators are nearly there now, close enough that they can hear the crack of the lanyards in the wind against the flagpoles above them, each with a flag of one of the 200 plus nations represented at the Games, the new flags bright and vivid and exotic. They start to queue for a final ticket and security check before entering the stadium itself together with a few members of international teams, wearing their official issue tracksuits, with the Swoosh or the stripes logos, and BOTSWANA, or JAPAN, or even USA stitched between their shoulder blades, adding to the sense that this is something international, and important.

Our father gives a second glance at one of the tracksuited athletes. He thinks he might half-recognise him from television... In fact, he's sure he is the American who was winning all those gold medals in the swimming pool earlier in the week. Now if he has come to the stadium tonight for this one race, it must be good, the father tells himself, still trying to think how he'll ever justify how he spent £1,200 on four tickets to see one man run in a race that won't last even ten seconds.

And then they are in, past the chap on the gate and now directed up and upwards, towards their appointed seats in the upper tier. It is when they emerge from the shade of the staircase and concrete corridor, out on to the concourse close under the stretched awning of the bright, white roof, that their moment finally arrives.

The girl looks down and smiles. The little boy is no longer distracted by the sideshows, because he has arrived at the main event. 'Look mummy!' he points. 'Just look!'

Now he is able to see the Olympic Stadium, all surrounded by swatches of multi-coloured seats, very many of them already occupied even though there is still an hour before the first event, nearly two before the runner they are all here to see is supposed to make his first appearance of the night. The green of the infield looks greener than any grass they have ever seen before. The white of the painted lines between the lanes of the running track is so bold it looks as if it is raised up, inches off the ground.

At each end of the stadium, a vast video screen is re-running some of the action from the morning session, pumping out at high volume the official Olympic pop song which Adele had sung to billions on the night of the opening ceremony a few nights before. And there at the end of the straight, just a few feet in on the infield, is the electronic clock, by which everything will be judged.

Of course, there are people, the aficionados, who are there to marvel at the athleticism of the triple jumpers or the balletic skills of the discus throwers. But on this night there is only one contest that probably 75,000 of the 80,000 paying spectators truly care about: who is the world's fastest man?

Such is the impact of Usain Bolt that, when tickets for the 2012 Olympics went on sale, first the computer system crashed (although the organisers soon had it up and running again), and then certain key sports sessions sold out immediately. In athletics, the evening session of Sunday, August 5, proved particularly popular. Indeed, in Britain alone, one in twenty of all tickets applications received by LOCOG, the London Organising Committee for the Olympic and Paralympic Games, was specifically to see Jamaica's Usain Bolt run in the final of the 100 metres that evening.

Usain Bolt is the man who has saved athletics.

IT WAS IN 2003 that I had my first encounter with Usain Bolt. We were in Sherbrooke, a small town in Canada that no one would find cause to visit unless they had to. It was the archetypal one-horse town, and the horse had left long ago. In Bolt's case he was there because he had been entered for two of the three sprint distances at the third World Youth Championships that were being staged at the Sherbrooke University track, and he would probably have to do relay duty, too, in due course. In my case, I was there because someone was paying me.

There was no doubt that Bolt was the star turn of the four-day meeting, a sporting superstar in the making as far as the people who run the sport of athletics were concerned.

'He's really very special,' a senior official of the world athletics governing body, the International Association of Athletics Federations, or IAAF, confided to me over an over-priced glass of wine in Sherbrooke's only decent restaurant on the evening before the action was due to begin.

The official had seen Bolt a year earlier, when he had raced at the 2002 World Junior Championships staged in Kingston, Jamaica. That venue had been chosen in a previous century, long before even Bolt's own mother, or his teachers at Piedmont Basic School in his rural home town of Trelawny, could have predicted his prodigious sprinting abilities. So it was the sport's immense good fortune, a trick of good timing, that Usain Bolt would be unveiled on the international stage in front of thousands of adoring Jamaicans.

At just fifteen years of age, Bolt experienced for the first time the sort of mass hysteria effect that he can have on a crowd. And it scared him so much he nearly ran the most important race of his life thus far with his spiked shoes on the wrong feet.

In the event, Bolt managed to get his shoes on to the right feet, get to his starting blocks in the third lane, run in a 200 metres race and win it in 20.61 seconds, ending with everyone in the 33,000-strong crowd on their feet, chanting his name, as if he had scored the winning goal in injury time at Old Trafford:

'Usain!'
'Usain!'
'Usain!'

Bolt was world junior champion, the youngest athlete ever to win a global under-20s title. His rivals that day? Wes Felix? Brendan Christian? Sebastian

Ernst? None are likely to be on the start line of the Olympic final in London in 2012, such is the fleeting nature of athletics talent, such is the high drop-out rate, even among kids good enough to be among the best eight in the world before their twentieth birthdays.

Even then, Bolt was very tall, but reed-thin, a schoolboy standing head and shoulders above the students and young men he was competing against. Bolt has recently described that humid night in his capital city as 'the one and only time I've felt real pressure'. He had gone into the competition ranked the fifth fastest junior in the world that season – not at all bad in an age group for those aged up to nineteen – and then he got lucky. The older, more experienced, stronger and speedier teenagers ranked first, second, third and fourth never made it to Kingston. 'The less challengers the better as far as I was concerned,' Bolt said.

In his ghosted autobiography published in 2010, Bolt recalled: 'Having got through to the 200m final, I was extremely nervous walking out through the tunnel into our national stadium. The crowd were cheering... the place went ballistic.

'I was a kid of fifteen and the enormity of it hit me. I cannot recall feeling so much pressure in my life. I had never been in a situation like this before.'

For anyone who has not competed in top-level sport, it is impossible to imagine how a teenager from a quiet country town might feel when placed in such a spotlight, the focus of so much attention and expectation. The Kingston crowd probably didn't care that this was his debut international championship, that he was three or four years younger than those in the racing lanes either side of him, who had had three or four years more training and work in the gym. All they knew was that Bolt was Jamaican and they wanted him, expected him, to win.

Maybe that just made the pressure even worse: the fear of failure is a terrible thing.

It was only after the starter's gun had sounded and as he began to do what he does best – run – that Bolt felt the tension drain away from his body. Geoffrey Green's theory of how a sports stadium can be transformed into an arena for energy transference was put to the test that night in Kingston.

Now the support of the crowd began to work for Bolt in a positive manner, a wave of energy carrying him down the home straight, passing the other runners and crossing the finishing line well clear of his closest rival.

'He's really very special,' the official repeated over our coffees almost a year later, the stage for the drama no one can foretell having been transplanted to eastern Canada.

'But what's his best event?' I asked, curious as to how for such a tall young man, his long levers of legs, might unwrap themselves in a 200-metre sprint if he had the misfortune, as must surely be the case one day, to be drawn in, say, lane one, or even lane two, where the tightness of the bend would certainly hinder his progress.

In Sherbrooke, the competition was spread out over four days, Thursday to Sunday. At senior international athletics championships the various events are spaced out over perhaps as many as nine days, with qualifying rounds usually staged in morning sessions, and finals scheduled for the evenings, when the biggest crowds would be in attendance. The World Youth Championships, however, are run much more like a glorified school sports day.

Anyone with ambitions of success in more than a single sprint event would need speed, obviously, but also strength and stamina to cope with multiple rounds and little rest time. In Sherbrooke, as well as his World Junior Championships event – the 200 metres – which had heats, and then both the semi-finals and finals on the last day of the meeting, Bolt had also been entered for the 400 metres, with a heat to race on the Thursday and the final on the Friday.

So just what might, ultimately, be Bolt's best distance? 'It might be the 400,' judged the official, himself a decent enough sprinter in his younger days, 'once he has worked on his strength, matured into his body. And stopped growing, too...' By repute, Bolt had grown another two inches since his victory in Kingston the year before.

'We're working with the Jamaican federation, though, to make sure he is looked after properly,' the IAAF official admitted. In the language of international sports officials, the word 'working' often implies money is involved in some manner.

'He'll be moving to Kingston, so that he can train properly, be coached properly, but so that he can get an education, too.

'He's important to the sport,' the official said, an added earnestness in his voice now. It was important that I understood the point he was about to make. 'He's the future of the sport.'

Could I speak to him? Would I get a chance to chat with Bolt some time over the course of the weekend? Interviewing teenagers, however important they might be to the future of any sport, is never easy. Few teenagers will speak openly with their own parents, never mind a complete stranger.

My dinner with the IAAF official was on the Wednesday evening. I had flown into Canada, via Montreal, the day before. After collecting my accreditation tag to wear around my neck for the next week, along with start sheets and the event handbook, I had sought out the British team management to put in a request to interview a couple of their rising stars.

Somewhat reluctantly, I gathered, the team manager said that I could get half an hour on Wednesday lunchtime with a young woman from Sheffield, called Jessica Ennis, who but for some dodgy javelin technique was thought to be quite a promising multi-eventer, and with a middle-distance runner from Liverpool called Michael Rimmer, who apart from sharing a name with a character in *Red Dwarf*, had a virtually unfathomable Scouse accent. So by the time of my dinner with the nice chap from the IAAF that evening, I still had plenty of space in my notebook for a piece on the living embodiment of the future of international athletics.

'We'll see,' my friendly official said, picking up the bill for our meal. 'I can't promise anything. He has a busy schedule the next couple of days, what with the 200 and the 400, and the relay as well.' In total, it was possible that Bolt would have to race seven times in four days. In 2003, there was no mention of Usain Bolt as a 100 metres runner.

As if his racing schedule was not enough in Sherbrooke, Bolt was even given the duty, the honour, of being flag-carrier at the opening ceremony. Every sports event, however minor or obscure, it seems, deems it an essential to have a parade of flags just like they have at the Olympics, and many of the athletes buy-in to the idea. Bolt, at 6ft 5in tall and with the black, gold and green flag of Jamaica waving high above his head, was no exception. 'I was very proud when I entered the stadium carrying the Jamaican flag,' he said. 'It was a great honour.'

As it turned out, the only chance I would get to speak to Bolt was immediately after that parade of flags at the opening ceremony. There could not have been a starker contrast to the media clamour for Bolt that was to come a few years later, as together with an American woman reporter, I persuaded him and his Jamaican team official minder to pause for a while in the shelter of the stadium's main stand, out of the wind and the rain which was to blight almost every day of the meeting.

So there we were, two reporters, plus one of the IAAF's own media staff, with the embodiment of the future of international track and field, each of us craning our necks upwards, hoping not to miss a word of what Bolt might say as he smiled affably enough, but spoke very softly and said very little.

Was he worried about the prospect of all these races in just four days? 'It's gonna be fine,' he almost whispered. 'I'm cool. I don't get stressed you know. It's just a question of being able to cope with the several races and I'm sure I will.'

What had he done differently in the past year? 'I have just been training hard. Nothing has changed, I have continued training like I always used to.'

Hardly the sort of stuff Woodward and Bernstein would have wanted. But at this stage it was an introduction in the hope that further opportunities might present themselves over the course of the next couple of days, and in the next few years.

But there was hardly an auspicious start to that project, as after routinely qualifying for the 400 metres final, Bolt was absent when the seven other runners took to their blocks on the Friday afternoon for what should have been his first medal race.

'A stomach bug' came the explanatory euphemism from the Jamaican team to the press stand. Would he be all right for the 200 metres tomorrow? All we got as an answer was a shrug. So much for our pre-prepared lines about a 'new Michael Johnson', capable of achieving what was generally regarded as an 'impossible' double of 200 and 400 metres titles at the same championships, as the American sprinter had managed at the 1996 Olympics in Atlanta. As well as our storylines, it seemed that the future of the sport was disappearing down a Canadian toilet.

The following morning Bolt was due to race in the very first track event of the day, the first heat of the 200 metres first round, at 10.05 am. There was a sense of relief when he was spotted warming up with a few casual strides down the back straight. And despite the unfavourable draw for such a tall man of lane two, he duly won the preliminary race in 21.12sec.

There was no formalised Mixed Zone at Sherbrooke, where journalists could question athletes as they left the stadium after the event, and it was not unusual for the youngsters to slip away untroubled by even the soft questions they were likely to receive from the rag-tag two dozen or so reporters attending the meeting.

Fortunately, someone did manage to speak to Bolt after his run. 'I was a little sick yesterday, so I couldn't run the 400 metres. But I took the medicine that they gave me and I now feel fine,' he said at the time.

Only years later did it emerge that there had been nothing wrong with Bolt at all, and that he had withdrawn from the 400 simply because he did not want to race it. 'I remember the competition more for the laughs with my friends,' Bolt admitted.

'I was supposed to run the 400 metres at the Youths as well but didn't want to – it would have got in the way of our fun,' he said.

'If you are entered for an event, you have to give a reason why you can't run, so there was nothing else for it, I had to fake a bout of diarrhoea.'

The only 'runs' Bolt had in Sherbrooke were in

the 200 metres, and we know now that it was the Jamaican's rivals who were probably sick of the sight of their giant rival, who they usually viewed only from the back.

The weather in Sherbrooke throughout the championships had been disappointingly chill and wet, with the sprinters often facing strong winds down the home straight, slowing their performances. By the time of the boys' 200 metres finals, the rain was lashing down, turning the track almost into a skid pan.

The official meeting report of that race relates:

'Usain Bolt duly added the World Youth 200 metres title to the World Junior title he won at the same distance a year ago in Kingston with a display of overwhelming power.

'With the final staged in atrocious conditions of rain and run into a 1.1 metre per second wind, Bolt, 1.99m (6ft 5in) and drawn in lane three, clearly had some trouble just holding the curve with his gigantic strides on the wet track.

'Yet he had overtaken the stagger within 80 metres on his biggest rival, Michael Grant, of the United States.

'Off the bend, Bolt was finally able to unravel his stride to best effect, and for the first time this week we saw the Jamaican teenager really turn on maximum effort. It is an awesome sight.

'Bolt stopped the clock at 20.40sec. Given better conditions, it cannot be long before Bolt dips inside 20sec – and the Jamaican selectors may now have to consider whether to include this precocious talent in their team for the senior World Championships in Paris next month.

'Behind Bolt, Grant achieved some compensation for his disqualification in the 100m semi-finals with a silver medal in 21.04, while nearly a full second behind the winner, Jamahl Alert-Khan, in 21.35, won Britain's third bronze medal of the championships.'

For Bolt, success over 200 metres was more than enough that week. He had opted out of running the 400 metres, albeit disingenuously, demonstrating well enough even at a tender age that he wanted to be master of his own destiny. Though that, to some extent at least, had already been decided for him.

Nevertheless, two world titles in two years and all before his seventeenth birthday. Maybe he truly was the future of the sport.

Chapter 2

Get Set

IT IS MORE than a sixty-mile drive from Kingston, Jamaica's capital, on a route that first winds northwards across the island and then west parallel with the coast, on sometimes narrow and hilly roads through thick, tropical countryside, to the parish of Trelawny. You could almost be driving back in time.

Named after an eighteenth century British governor of the island, Trelawny, now, as then, has sugar cane as its staple crop. And therein lies at least part of the explanation for another significant, more modern product of Jamaica: sprinters.

'Natural selection' of the most hideous kind, through the slave trade which populated the cane fields with young men and women forcibly stolen from west Africa, and then two centuries of generation after generation undertaking back-breaking, hard, manual labour, chopping and hacking at the sugar cane from before dawn, six days a week, has resulted in near-domination of 21st-century international sprinting by Jamaicans, men and women.

When asked by *Sports Illustrated* magazine to explain why black Americans produced so extraordinarily disproportionate a number of the highest-class athletes in the world the 1968 Olympic 400 metres champion Lee Evans emphasised this point. 'We were bred for it. Certainly the black people who survived in the slave ships must have contained a high proportion of the strongest. Then, on the plantations, a strong black man was mated with a strong black woman. We were simply bred for physical qualities.'

The dominance has switched from the USA to Jamaica but Evans' argument is still valid.

The island nation of Jamaica is just 145 miles long and fifty miles wide, with a population of less than three million. Yet men born in Jamaica have managed to cross the finishing line first in the 100 metres at four of the last six Olympic Games. Three of those runners had emigrated from Jamaica when young boys and grown up elsewhere in the world, so the explanation for such global dominance can hardly be the facilities or training regime used in Kingston. It is innate sprinting talent, power and strength.

Even a quiet backwater such as the parish of Trelawny has produced a set of champions worthy of an all-star track and field team: Veronica Campbell-Brown, Michael Frater, Michael Green, Debbie-Ann Parris, Sanya Richards... and, of course, Usain Bolt.

Bolt was born in Trelawny on August 21, 1986, the son of Wellesley and Jennifer. It is to Trelawny, back to his mother and father, his half-brother and half-sister, and the rest of the family, that Bolt withdraws whenever he is feeling stressed – usually about business, appearances and girls, he says, 'not track and field, which never worries me'.

'Back home I'll stay at Mom and Dad's in Coxheath near Sherwood Content, go round to Aunty Lilly's, visit my grandmother, and meet up with the guys who were my friends from way back when we played cricket together on the road outside our front door,' Bolt wrote in his 2010 ghosted biography, where he spoke about using the stump of a banana tree for a wicket, and playing dominoes on the porch of the house late into the night. 'Life doesn't get any simpler,' he said.

It is a paradox that the world's fastest man can come from a tiny village where everything moves so slowly. It has been said that there are days in Sherwood Content when the only thing that seems to be moving is the smoke rising from the nearby cane fields.

To find Sherwood Content, you turn off the road near Falmouth (the main town in Trelawny, given a suitably Cornish name by its Cornish founder nearly 250 years ago) and drive inland away from the beaches along a narrow road pitted with potholes.

There are no road signs and rarely are the houses or buildings numbered. A stranger looking to find a particular house has to wind down the window and call out to passersby. They all know where Usain Bolt lived, though.

And once in the village, it is easy enough to find the general store run by Wellesley Bolt, which he bought with redundancy money when laid off from his job with a Falmouth coffee company. Nearby is the pink bungalow with a porch in front and a satellite dish on top, where the world's fastest man, the future of athletics, was brought up. In the past couple of years, a part of Usain Bolt's fortune has been used to pay for improvements to the family home, including building an extension.

The heat and rich soil around Trelawny ensure that the plants, yams and coffee beans as well as sugar, grow fast and grow tall. In Bolt's case, he grew tall and fast as well.

Like most Jamaican children, when Bolt played it was often outdoors, football if not cricket, and his parents remember him as a particularly energetic child. They worried, as all parents do about their children, and they took Usain to the doctor because he could never stay still.

'I was all over the place, climbing things,' Bolt said in an interview in 2010. 'My mum goes, "There must be something wrong with this kid", and the doctor goes, "Nooooo, he's just hyperactive." '

His mother, a Seventh Day Adventist, was gentle and forgiving, his father a disciplinarian. 'Manners is the key thing,' Bolt says of his upbringing. 'Say, for instance, when you're growing up, you're walking down the street, you've got to tell everybody "Good morning." Everybody. You can't pass one person.'

Hyperactive Usain was taken on at the local Piedmont Basic School when aged just two, almost eighteen months younger than most children begin there. 'His parents thought he was ready, and that he was,' Sheron Seivwright, the school's head teacher recalled. 'Usain was so full of energy when he entered school, always running around the classroom and impossible to catch.'

Seivwright remembers young Usain as being tall for his age, good at his lessons ('his handwriting was absolutely beautiful') and clearly talented in physical education classes. Aged six, Bolt duly moved to Waldensia Primary, where again he is remembered for always doing his homework, and where his mother was chairwoman of the Parent-Teachers' Association.

Waldensia has a grass track next door where they stage their school sports day, and it was here that Usain Bolt, aged six and running barefoot, made his formal athletics debut. They do not use chalk dust or paint to mark out the lanes at Waldensia, but diesel, which is poured on to the grass and set alight, to burn brown lines for the track.

By the age of ten, Bolt was sprinting for his primary school team, and his mother says that by the time he was twelve, 'he was beating everybody', representing his school in the 100 metres in annual primary schools' meeting for Trelawny parish. In one meeting on a grass track elsewhere on the island, Bolt was timed at 52.0sec for 400 metres at the age of 12.

The man who would sign a £21 million, five-year deal in 2010 to help to promote a German sportswear brand's sales of £60-a-pair running shoes did not possess any such footwear himself until after his thirteenth birthday. 'When you're growing up,' Bolt once said, 'you can't afford spikes.'

Into his teens, Bolt played less football, and less cricket, and was doing more running, and more seriously too. He had moved schools, to William Knibb High, where he began to receive more structured coaching from Pablo McNeil, a former Olympic sprinter, and Darland Clarke, as well as others.

'THEY SAID, TRY track and field, and I continued because it was easy and I was winning,' Bolt said. And athletics' gain is almost certainly cricket's loss. Imagine the pace of a Michael Holding delivered from the height of Joel Garner: Bolt the bowler would have terrified batsmen around the world.

'The first time I saw Usain bowling I knew he was a born sprinter, he was so fast,' McNeil said in a 2008 interview with the *Observer* newspaper. 'But he was so cricket-mad that he took a bit of persuading. Initially he was quite hard to work with, he needed to be kept in line ... nothing malicious, just pranks that got a bit out of hand, he certainly kept you on your toes.

'I knew a long time that he was a cut above the rest. He's got an incredible stride, which just eats up the ground. I'm not in the least bit surprised at what he is achieving because I predicted five or six years ago that he was going to break world records. Anyone who saw him as a kid wouldn't have needed to be a prophet to tell you that.'

As if reinforcing McNeil's long-held faith in Bolt's abilities, it has become part of the legend that now surrounds the sprinter that during training sessions, one coach refused to allow the runner to see the stopwatch that had been timing his efforts, for fear that the runner would get big-headed, or perhaps become lazy because of the ease with which he was able to run phenomenal times.

Dwight Barnett, one of the PE teachers at William Knibb, said, 'Sometimes I'd look at that stop-watch and think, "There's something wrong with this watch. No kid can run that quickly." '

And after all, it was not as if the young Bolt did not have distractions or behave like any other teenager away from the track. His parents, despite being far from wealthy, bought their son a Nintendo games console, mainly because it allowed them to know exactly where Usain could be found – in their living room with maybe nine or ten friends at a time. Wellesley Bolt even instituted a 10 pm curfew on his son in an effort to rein him in. Yet more than once, with an important training session planned, one of Usain's track coaches at school had to take a taxi to retrieve their errant charge from Falmouth, where he had gone to flirt with some girls.

Being so tall, Bolt was easily noticed when he was on the track. 'I first saw Usain when he was thirteen years old,' Stephen Francis, one of Jamaica's leading coaches, recalls, having spotted the youngster at Jamaica's annual schools championships, where up to 2,000 boys and girls compete each year. 'A skinny, tall guy. I doubted whether he would make the transition. I figured he would be trying to go abroad. I figured he would be lost like so many others before him,' Francis said.

Jamaica has been a long-time rich recruiting ground for colleges in America, which often have generous budgets to offer scholarships to promising young sportsmen and women, who are lured by the chance of getting a degree education thanks to their physical talents. American college competitions often feature a variety of relay races as well as standard sprints, making versatile sprinters who can run several events particularly attractive signings for them.

But US colleges are also notorious for chewing up and spitting out promising track talents, who perhaps because of the conditions of their scholarships are forced, or at the very least feel obliged, to over-race and over-train, to the point where they may suffer long-term injuries and burn-out.

It was this concern that, once Bolt had won his first world junior title in 2003, prompted the IAAF, track and field's world governing body, to discuss with the Jamaican national body ways of nurturing this delicate talent.

There were even letters in the Jamaican national press about young Usain's future: 'It is the responsibility of the JAAA' – meaning the Jamaican Amateur Athletic Association – 'to ensure that this new found treasure receives nurturing and protection. Usain Bolt is the most phenomenal sprinter ever produced by this island and history will judge them harshly if they fail,' Howard Hamilton, a senior government lawyer, wrote to the *Kingston Observer*.

While the consensus was that they wanted to keep Bolt based in Jamaica, in truth, they did not have to do too much persuading.

'I wanted to go home, I was so homesick,' Bolt said of his first overseas trip for an international competition, when as a fourteen-year-old he flew to Barbados to compete against sixteen-year-olds in a Caribbean regional age group championships, finishing second in both the 200 and 400 metres.

By contrast, Bolt would later describe the international jet-set lifestyle of his teenaged athletics years, travelling to different places for competitions, as 'like going on your holidays'. Yet the idea of moving to the United States full-time once his high school career was over never seemed to appeal, despite the blandishments of the American colleges. Bolt turned down at least half a dozen scholarship offers.

Stephen Francis, who was coaching another top Jamaican sprinter, Asafa Powell, observed the preferential treatment Bolt received after his victory at the World Junior Championships in Kingston. 'Suddenly, he was a big star. He got a lot of encouragement from the federation who wanted him to stay in Jamaica. Usain had everything possible done for him to keep him from going abroad.'

Jamaican track officials sought to recruit a mentor, someone who could provide Bolt with one-on-one supervision, both on his studies and for his training. After liaising with Margaret Lee, the principal at William Knibb High School, it was decided to approach Norman Peart – a former pupil and athlete, who was working in the tax office at Montego Bay.

'The principal called and said there was a special athlete she wanted me to consider,' Peart remembered. 'When I enquired about Usain, I was told he was obedient and talented, two great attributes I looked for in people generally.' After meeting with the Bolt family, and being impressed by his father and mother, Peart decided 'to take on Usain as a project'.

It was not long before Peart got the chance to see his new 'project' in action on the track. 'Do I have an Olympic champion on my hands?' was Peart's first reaction.

Later in 2003, the decision was made to bow to the inevitable and allow Bolt to become a full-time athlete. He left school to train at Jamaica's high-performance centre on the other side of the island ('I joined the big world,' Bolt recalled, 'moved to Kingston and became a professional athlete'). Bolt even moved into an apartment in Kingston with Peart, who was acting *in loco parentis*. The working partnership has continued ever since, with Peart most recently acting as Bolt's personal manager.

Peart's 'project' saw him seek other personnel for Team Bolt: Fitz Coleman was to be the new, sole coach; two tutors worked with Bolt to help him pass the minimum qualifications for college entry; and a deal was done with a specialist sports agency which had been founded in the 1980s in south-west London, PACE Sports management, to represent the runner's interests in negotiations with meeting organisers around the world.

By the end of 2003, Bolt even had his own endorsement contract, with Puma, the German-based sportswear firm which already had very strong ties with the Jamaican national team.

But what had seemed to be a timeline of untrammelled progress and success now turned into almost four years of pain, self-doubt and the discovery of a career-threatening condition, as Bolt's life as a professional athlete suffered a massive false start.

Olympic year 2004 had begun so promisingly, too, as an early-season race in Bermuda saw Bolt underline his massive promise when, at the age of seventeen, he took 0.14sec off the world junior record for 200 metres, running 19.93sec to go top of the year's world rankings ahead of the Athens Games.

Behind the scenes, it was not all sweetness and light in Team Bolt. Throughout his fledgling athletics career, Bolt had always trained and raced as a 200–400 metres runner, something which required all his natural speed, but would also see him undertake some gruelling training sessions running repetitions of 300, 400, 500 and even 600 metres.

By 2004, however, much of this was being done with the runner suffering increasing amounts of back pain. Bolt became disillusioned with the coaching of Coleman: there was no solution to his pain, and a hamstring pull was followed by an injury to his Achilles tendon. 'Coleman was determined that I should go to the Olympics, hamstring troubles or not,' Bolt said.

Bolt felt he was unprepared for the Olympics, and he'd have preferred to have spent 2004 focusing on defending his world junior title at 200 metres. 'My workload was too much, I was being pushed too hard.' He has referred to his debut experience at the

Olympics as 'a complete waste of time'. Disenchanted, disinterested, almost not trying, in his 200 metres first-round heat at the Athens Olympics, Bolt placed only fifth, and failed to progress to the next round.

In Kingston, the change in surroundings and lifestyle was also forcing the teenager to make a lot of adjustments. The lure of the city, and the change from the regular meals of his mother's wholesome home cooking, were something which even Norman Peart could not monitor all the time.

Elton Tucker, a senior journalist on *The Gleaner*, Jamaica's biggest-selling newspaper, who has followed Bolt's career from its beginnings, says, 'When Bolt moved to Kingston he was looking at the bright lights – where he came from there were no street lights. Suddenly there was Burger King and KFC.

'Bolt was from a poor family, just ordinary country folk. He saw Asafa driving BMWs and Mercedes-Benz and he wanted that.

'As a teenager, Bolt wasn't focused, he liked nightclubs, playing basketball, he thought he could run on natural talent alone.'

In a 2011 interview Bolt has admitted that he used to enjoy nightclubs, parties and bottled Guinness. 'I was really bad, because I wasn't really focused yet. I'd go all night. But I never got drunk. I don't do drunk,' he said.

While at the Athens Olympics, living in the Athletes' Village and doing some training sessions with the Jamaican national squad, Bolt had seen at close hand the work of another coach, Glen Mills.

Mills had years of experience coaching world-class sprinters – he had guided the relatively unheralded Kim Collins, from St Kitts and Nevis, to the 100 metres world title in 2003, beating all the better-fancied Americans and Europeans.

'He discussed things with his athletes and worked with them,' Bolt observed. 'He didn't just tell you what to do like a teacher in class.'

As Bolt tells the story, he decided himself to approach Mills and asked him to take him on, leaving it to Peart to negotiate with Coleman. It was a decision that was to turn Bolt's career around.

'He understands that I'm lazy and that I might miss training,' Bolt has admitted. 'That's how I am. He doesn't get mad with me, he lets it go, but if I'm absent from more than one day's training, he will be ringing me asking me what's up and why I've not been there.'

These days, Usain Bolt very rarely misses any training sessions without good cause and advance notice. He cannot afford to, since each session is now preceded by at least an hour's aggressive massage therapy. To the uninitiated, it looks more like a form of torture, with Bolt on a massage table at the mercy of his physiotherapist, who bends his legs and his back this way and that, forcing the sprinter into wholly unnatural-looking contortions.

The treatment is what is helping to keep Usain Bolt on track, for now at least. When Mills took over as Bolt's coach at the end of 2004, he sent the sprinter away for medical and biomechanical analysis. It turned out that Bolt has a curvature of the spine which has made his right leg half an inch shorter than his left – not great for anyone, but especially not for someone who spends much of his working day running anti-clockwise around a track, with his longer, left leg on the inside on every bend.

The first medical examination diagnosed a condition called scoliosis, where the spine curves from one side to the other in an 'S' shape. As well as shortening his right leg, it was this imbalance in Bolt's body that was creating his hamstring injuries. To make matters worse, as Bolt would instinctively seek to compensate for the spinal curve and leg imbalance, he was also creating injury problems elsewhere in his body.

Scoliosis occurs in about two per cent of the population. Noticed in young children, it can be corrected through rigorous physiotherapy and the use of corrective braces. If not corrected and allowed to degenerate over time, sufferers can develop serious breathing problems.

In an Olympic-standard sprinter, such a condition is career-ending. At least that was his doctor's initial prognosis after examining Bolt. But Mills knew of a sometimes controversial doctor based in Munich, Germany, called Hans-Wilhelm Muller-Wohlfahrt. For forty years, Muller-Wohlfahrt has been the official team doctor to the Bayern Munich football club and to the national team, as well as working on an array of world stars from sport, including tennis player Boris Becker and marathon runner Paula Radcliffe, and even Bono, the lead singer of rock band U2.

Muller-Wohlfahrt combines conventional medical practice with homeopathic practices, notably using a series of injections of extracts from the crests of cockerels, calf foetuses and honey.

The detail of Bolt's treatment at the Munich clinic is not known, but the sprinter is certainly satisfied that the German doctor's therapies have helped.

Slowly, Bolt began to work his way back up the world rankings lists. His progress was not without setbacks, such as in 2005 at the World Championships in Helsinki. All week during the championships, enough rain fell on the Finnish capital to have persuaded Noah to get his boat-building kit out again.

The conditions were far from ideal for a 6ft 5in tall man from the warm Caribbean with an aching back and a dodgy hamstring. Although Bolt managed to make it through to the 200 metres final – his first at a senior international championships – he found himself drawn in lane one. The cold, wet weather, and several delays at the start, saw him suffer cramp sixty metres from the finish, forcing the Jamaican to jog across the line. A visit to Muller-Wohlfahrt in Munich soon afterwards also discovered a small tear in Bolt's troublesome hamstring.

Nonetheless, Bolt, by now nineteen, was encouraged. He managed to run sub-20sec again in a 200 metres race at London's Crystal Palace that season, too.

The following year, despite public pressure in Jamaica for him to represent his country at the Commonwealth Games staged in Melbourne, Bolt and

Mills agreed he would be better not to endure too intense a summer track season in Europe. After years of racing fast in April and May, then breaking down in June and July, in 2006 Bolt managed to produce some of his best performances at the business-end of the track season. Against world-class senior opposition, he placed third at 200 metres in one meeting in Germany and a week later in Athens finished runner-up at the World Cup.

Bolt spent the 2007 European track season trying to make up for lost time, taking on as many races as he could, not just for the experience of senior competition at the highest level, but also for the cash. After a couple of lean years, he needed to start earning his keep and also satisfy his sponsors.

His main event, though, the 200 metres, was not often on the programme at the major meetings, usually because promoters preferred the sprinters to race the Blue Riband of the track, the 100 metres.

Bolt found this frustrating, especially when he watched his Jamaican relay teammate, Asafa Powell, by now the 100 metres world record-holder, raking in the dough. For winning a 100 metres race in Brussels, Paris or Zurich, Bolt realised that Powell was banking £10,000, on top of any appearance money deal. In 2006, Powell even took the lion's share of the $750,000 Golden League season's jackpot.

Bolt clearly wanted a slice of this action, but his coach still believed he ought to be racing 400 metres races as well as the 200, and not the 100. Just as in 2003, when he had the 'stomach bug' that never was to get out of running the 400 metres at the

World Youth Championships, Bolt did not fancy the prospect of racing the one-lap event.

He needed to demonstrate to his coach that he could, indeed, be competitive over 100 metres, and so they entered him for a race at a minor meet in Crete, the Vardinoyiannia in Rethymno.

If Bolt managed to run well, Mills promised that he would be able to try 100s and 200s the following year; if he did not impress, the coming winter would be spent doing the sort of hard work necessary to race 400s as well as the 200. Bolt calls the quarter-milers' training 'severely hard': 'I don't think I'm made for so much work in one day,' he said.

The history of track and field, the future of athletics, was changed forever when Bolt raced 100 metres that day. Bolt ran 10.03sec. He would get his way the following year.

It is possibly difficult to reconcile with his public persona that is so well known today, but there was more than a hint of self-doubt about Usain Bolt before his twenty-first birthday. All that promise, all that talent that he had shown when fourteen, fifteen and sixteen ... even he was wondering whether he would ever fulfil his potential.

It was at the World Championships, in Osaka, Japan, in late August 2007, that Bolt had his coming of age.

The American, Tyson Gay, had won the 100 metres final earlier in the championships, and he was drawn in lane four for the final, with Bolt, as the second fastest qualifier, put in the lane outside him. As the runners came off the bend and into the straight, Gay was already three metres up on Bolt, as hard as the young Jamaican was trying, the effort shown in the stressed sinews around his neck and shoulders as he sought to find every last ounce of speed from his torso.

At the finish line, Gay stopped the clock at 19.76sec, the fastest time ever seen in the twenty-four-year history of the World Championships. Bolt was second in 19.91, well clear of another American, Wallace Spearmon, in 20.05.

'I'd shown, at last, that I could produce in a major championships,' Bolt said, the grin on his face as he crossed the line symbolic of the relief he must have felt after three wretchedly troubled years. 'It wasn't until that silver in Japan that it struck me I could be a great athlete.'

Now with his coach's permission to train for 100 and 200 metres races, Usain Bolt looked forward to returning to Asia in twelve months' time. Because the next time he would be running in a championship event would be at the Beijing Olympic Games.

Chapter 3

Go!

'I JUST BLEW my mind,' Usain Bolt said. He was speaking to a sweaty pressroom outside the Bird's Nest Stadium in Beijing in which there was standing room only for the journalists, photographers and camera crews from nearly 200 countries. It was almost midnight in China, but thanks to Bolt, most of the world was wide awake.

'I just blew my mind': it was probably the most modest thing he had said, or done, in the previous week. For in the course of a just a few days at the 2008 Beijing Olympic Games, Usain Bolt had managed to blow the world's mind, and change the course of international sport for ever.

Bolt had gone from being the teenager who had been looked upon, almost in desperation by some sports officials, as the future of international athletics, to the man who was making history. He had won Olympic gold in the 100 metres in world record time. He had won gold in the 200 metres, again faster than any man had ever run before. And when given the chance to help three Jamaican teammates get their little bit of Beijing glory in the 4x100 metres relay, from a rolling start Bolt had run faster still. Three golds, three world records.

Yet Bolt had very nearly not even entered the race which was to be the fulcrum of this Olympic triptych, the race which carried with it the title of 'the world's fastest man'.

Having performed so well when running his first 100 metres race as a senior the year before, the sometimes headstrong and self-confessed 'lazy' athlete had done a deal with his coach, Glen Mills, to let him double up and race the 100 and 200 metres in 2008. After all, the money was better, and most importantly, it meant no 400 metres races, or training.

Bolt would need to race his best event, the 200 metres, of course, and although he had won the silver medal in the 'deuce' at the 2007 World Championships, he would still be expected to earn his Olympic selection for the Jamaican team at the national championships in Kingston at the end of June.

He might even have a run out in his new distance there, too, if his coach agreed, although before the season began, few would have predicted that Bolt, with the relatively modest lifetime best of 10.03sec, would have much of a chance in the shorter sprint against Jamaica's more experienced 100-metre men, many of whom were rated among the world's best.

Top of that list was Asafa Powell, like Bolt one of Jamaica's 'country boys', but who had made the move to Kingston and the big time in track and field. More than once, Bolt had remarked on how he liked the look of Powell's very smart Mercedes-Benz, bought and paid for with the proceeds of his appearance fees, prize money and six-figure record bonuses from his sponsors.

Four times Powell had set the world record for the dash, most recently in a race in Italy the previous September. After placing a disappointing third in the 100 metres final at the World Championships in Japan, Powell had scorched another 0.03sec off his own record, establishing 9.74sec as the fastest for the Blue Riband event. The 100 metres world record was only ever revised by tiny splinters of a second.

And then came Usain Bolt.

Although now in his twenties, Bolt was still willowy slim. His back problems and the changeover in coaches had meant that for the previous two or three winters, the 'off-season' when most athletes do much of their hard training, he had done little of the intensive gym work so beloved of most sprinters. Only after returning from Osaka, and a brief break from training in October 2007, did Bolt return to training with more weights work on his schedule. But even then, caution over his scoliosis meant that such sessions were limited.

As well as lacking the upper body bulk conventionally associated with the powerhouses in the event, Bolt's height was also thought to work against him in the shortest sprint, being four or five inches taller than what was considered the 'optimum' for a 100-metre sprinter. He would take so long unravelling his long legs after the starter's gun fired, most observers reckoned, that the race would be lost for him in the first twenty or thirty metres.

In the spring of 2008, as he began to do more speed-focused training sessions, Coach Mills was looking ever more carefully at Bolt's starting technique. It was all good practice, they figured, because if he improved his start and was quicker away from his blocks, it would only help his 200-metre running, surely?

Bolt entered another 100 metres in April, an early season pipe-opener, and then it was arranged for him to race in an invitation meeting on May 3 at the National Stadium in Kingston, the same track where Bolt had been acclaimed so fondly six years before when he had won the world junior title at 200 metres.

It would be the toughest test yet of Bolt's 100-metre potential, the organisers having lined up his American 200-metre rival, Wallace Spearmon, and Darvis Patton against him. Anything sub-10sec would be good, Team Bolt reasoned, as it would put him among the world class at a second event.

Bolt ran 9.76sec.

The manner of his running was instructive: the starting block drills had worked, and Bolt was not left at a disadvantage over the early strides. But once he had worked through his 'pick up', raising himself to his full height and using his full stride length, Bolt seemed to accelerate away from the halfway mark. He even seemed to ease up before the finishing line.

The 12,000-strong crowd took to their feet to hail their rediscovered hero as he jogged a lap of honour, his own incredulity at what he had just done barely disguised. Was the timing equipment working properly? Had the wind gauge malfunctioned?

Everything, of course, was entirely in order, even the following wind, of 1.8 metres per second, slightly less than the 2.0 metres per second tolerance allowed for sprint times to be recognised for record purposes before they are considered 'wind assisted'. Bolt, the 100 metres novice, had just come within two-hundredths of a second of the world record in only his third race at the distance.

'Our minds were made up that I would run both the 100 and 200 metres at the Beijing Olympics,' he said in his 2010 biography.

At the time, Bolt struck local reporters as being less decisive about his course of action. 'Shocked' was one word used to describe the world's newest sprint star's reaction to his own run.

'I knew I was coming here to do under ten seconds as my training was going pretty well,' Bolt told the handful of journalists. 'I really did not know I was going that fast.'

Could he go faster? Faster even than Powell's world record, the reporters asked, perhaps hoping that they might instigate some sort of Bolt v Powell rivalry that would convince their editors that sending them to China later in the year for the Beijing Olympics would be worthwhile.

'Oh, I don't know,' Bolt answered, deflating the headline expectations of the reporters. 'The night was just right, everything was just perfect. You never know, this might just be one good race, but I am hoping it is not.'

Watching from the trackside that night was Tyson Gay, the double world champion, who had raced the 200 metres earlier in the evening. 'That 100 metres was amazing,' the American said.

Gay would soon enough get to race against Bolt himself, as the Jamaican's latest performance had just catapulted him on to every track meeting promoter's 'must-have' list for track's phoney war build-up to the Olympic Games.

Among the first on the phone to Bolt's London-based agents were the organisers of a Grand Prix meeting to be staged in New York at the end of May. They were offering Bolt the biggest appearance fee of his career, with the proviso that he would have to line up against Tyson Gay, the 100 metres world champion and the whole of America's favourite to win gold in Beijing later in the year.

The deal was swiftly done. 'If the athletics world had doubts about me, this was the place to put them right,' Bolt said.

Bolt took in one more 100 metres race, in Port of Spain a couple of weeks later, where he proved his Kingston run was not a fluke, or a one-off, as he underlined his sub-10sec credentials with a 9.92sec run. Respectable enough, but nothing likely to intimidate Gay as he waited for his moment in New York.

The New York meeting promoters, in true showman style, scheduled the men's 100 metres to be the climax of the night. The track at Randall's Island is fast enough: Leroy Burrell had set a 100 metres world record there back in 1991. But with track and field not being a major sport in the United States, the stadium itself is a little run-down, frayed at the edges.

That, however, did not deter the thousands of spectators who rolled up that night, many of them Jamaican ex-pats living in New York. So many turned out that the organisers had to put up 'Sold Out' signs hours before the meeting started, while dozens of spectators were allowed in to take up standing room down the back straight.

The one thing no meeting organiser can control, though, is the weather, and the muggy night in New York produced heavy rain and an electrical storm. After an initial hour's delay to the start of the meeting, midway through athletes, officials and spectators had to take cover for another forty minutes as forked lightning threatened over the arena.

Once the storm had blown over, volunteers came out to help brush away the standing water and puddles from the home straight. All was soon ready for the main event.

Bolt, gangling, wearing a white Puma vest, was picked out in the weak floodlights before the start. Gay, in his usual pre-race routine, prowled around the blocks, impatient for the race.

Even when the gun did fire, a second shot came straight after as the starter recalled the field. One of the other runners, Mike Rodgers, was judged to have false-started. Neither Bolt nor Gay had got away particularly cleanly first time; now they would get another chance.

It was Bolt who started the better as Gay, slowly away, was left. 'I knew if I could beat Tyson out of the blocks, I could win the race,' Bolt said. Yet this 100 metres race was about so much more than just the start.

Watched over again, it is clear that Gay was unable to cope with Bolt's gigantic strides. Even though he got close to the Jamaican, he could never quite stay with him. Once Bolt's electric acceleration kicked for in the second half of the race, the world champion was left trailing.

Bolt's momentum took him past the finishing line and round into the back straight, where he started a joyous victory lap: he had just beaten the world champion! It was there that he heard his winning time announced: 'A world's record, 9.72 seconds!' Bolt beat his chest in delight and roared at the night sky.

Gay had run 9.85sec, within one-hundredth of his fastest ever, yet had been well beaten. 'We were on the same rhythm,' Gay said, 'but his stride was covering more ground. He's run 9.7 before, his body knows what it feels like.'

Both men attended a press conference afterwards, where Bolt tried not to sound too arrogant or dismissive. 'The world record means nothing without gold medals in the World Championships or the Olympics,' he said. 'If you are the Olympic champion, they have to wait four years to try to beat you.' He may not have intended to, but Bolt had just underlined the previous message he had given to Gay out on the track.

Bolt spent the rest of the summer assembling a set of 100 metres performances most sprinters would be proud to achieve over a lifetime. At the end of June, he won his place in Jamaica's team for the Olympics at 100 and 200 metres, winning national titles in both events, beating Powell to the former. Only once was Bolt beaten, towards the end of July, when he and Powell were brought together for a race in Stockholm – Powell ran 9.88, Bolt 9.89sec, an invisible sliver of time to the naked eye, but enough when analysed by the photo-finish equipment to add even more intrigue to the prospects in Beijing just three weeks later.

As in so many sports, psychological primacy is as important as physical supremacy in determining the outcome of major contests. That is why, outside of championship athletics meetings, rivals are rarely prepared to compete: if the time and place are right for one of them, the other may well find an excuse to race elsewhere, or try another event.

The European track season of 2008, therefore, had developed a fascinating narrative around the 100 metres: with the Olympic Games just weeks away, the man who had held the world record at the start of the year had been beaten by the man who had won the world title the previous year. Both had then been beaten by the new kid in the starting blocks, who also revised the world record. Then Tyson Gay beat Asafa Powell. Then Asafa Powell beat Usain Bolt.

Bolt, who had started the season with nothing to prove or fear as he tried out a new event, now joined the merry-go-round of rival-dodging which so often disfigures the European track circuit. He pulled out of what was supposed to be his last big race before Beijing, in London. 'Let's keep them confident,' his coach told Bolt.

What Mills had not told Bolt, though, was that he was about to announce that his charge would indeed race 100 and 200 metres in Beijing. It was hardly a well-kept secret – it would have been much more of a shock had Mills determined not to allow Bolt to go forward on the Jamaican Olympic committee's team sheet for both races.

But it was not until the week before the Games, at what one British reporter described as 'a bizarre and at times comically embarrassing press conference' staged by Bolt's shoe sponsors, that the position was confirmed, with one journalist informing the sprinter that his coach had sent an email to the Reuters news agency confirming that his Olympic double was on.

'I guess if he did say it, he didn't communicate it with me. That's the first time I've heard it actually,' said Bolt, who before he boarded the plane for China had recorded an answering machine message on his mobile phone proclaiming that he would win three gold medals in Beijing.

Puma, the shoe company, must have been given more notice, since at the end of the press conference they handed Bolt a pair of golden spikes with 'Beijing 100m' embroidered on them.

'It's the first miscommunication that I've ever had with my coach and I hope that it never happens again,' Bolt told the press. 'I have a good relationship with him. He's a father figure to me.'

Nor was it particularly bad news, as far as Bolt was concerned. By the time he checked in at the Athletes' Village in Beijing, he'd have heard that Gay – having bypassed the previous month's action due to a hamstring strain suffered at the US Olympic trials – was in town and ready to race. Being part of the same squad, he will have also known what sort of shape his teammate, Powell, was in. Bolt blamed his defeat to Powell in Stockholm, in any case, on a loss of concentration at the start. 'He was tightening up. I could've beaten him,' he reckoned. Now, they would all get to race together, on the same track, at the same time. 'I want to beat the best,' Bolt said.

And it was as if this was the stage that Bolt was always meant for. In Beijing, after a first week when the Olympic headlines had been dominated by swimmers, gymnasts, cyclists and rowers, the second week began with the focus on the Bird's Nest Stadium and the men's 100 metres.

The men had a morning start, with first-round heats which usually supply some of the biggest mismatches in international sport. A Polynesian shot-putter, unable to compete in his chosen event for lack of a qualifying distance, gets entered instead for the 100 (every country is allowed at least one competitor, in one event, at the Games; it's not the winning, but the taking part, after all), and lines up alongside the world record holder, and what we see is a 10.20sec jog versus 11.25sec, which the results computer helpfully informs the world is a personal best, perhaps even a national record.

The also-rans dispensed with before lunch, Bolt, Powell and Gay will have gone off for a warm-down, a massage possibly, and then some food and a sleep back in the Village, before a late afternoon call to take them back to the warm-up track to go through the process all over again at the evening session, and the quarter-finals.

Usually staged on a Saturday evening at global athletics championships, the second round of the 100 metres often provides the best insight into the sprinters' form and current psyche. No one likes to lose, but nor does anyone really want to show their hand too early. Bolt, for instance, won his quarter-final in 9.92sec, while Gay, after that month out of action, was only second in his quarter-final behind Trinidad's Richard Thompson, 9.99 to 10.09sec. Was he holding something back?

Such had been Bolt's transformation over the previous twelve months that for many, this was their first proper look at the lanky sprinter. Most were struck by the elegance of Bolt's running. 'How could he be so fast and yet so much at ease?' David Walsh, the *Sunday Times* features writer, asked. 'Other great sprinters pounded the track but he, the greatest of them all, glided over it. Bolt was a phenomenon.'

After the first two rounds, Bolt and his rivals would have again warmed down – important this, for they want no residual stiffness in their bodies in the morning. Eating soon enough after the race to refuel the body, and yet giving themselves time enough to digest it before they sleep, was also important.

In Bolt's case, this meant a visit to the branch of McDonald's in the Village and a bowl of chicken nuggets. Hardly the meal of champions, you might have thought, but 'I ate nothing else in all my time out in China ... They were the only food I could properly trust which wouldn't affect my stomach. Eat them I did, 15 at a time, for breakfast, lunch and dinner, washed down with bottled water.'

The heat and humidity of Beijing saw all the athletes try to drink plenty of fluids, too – their event may only last ten seconds, but two or three hours of warming up and down in a day is enough to cause race-ending cramp in the semi-final or final a day later.

Finals day for the 100 metres men usually allows them to sleep in – the semi-finals would be staged at the track early in the evening session, a tune-up for the final three hours or so later. An experienced athlete will know not to be up and about too soon anyway, fretting over the racing to come, exhausting themselves of nervous energy before they even arrive at the warm-up track to check in and find their lane assignments.

That Bolt meant business was clear enough in his semi-final, a 9.85sec victory, while minutes later Powell looked to be the biggest threat, winning the second semi in 9.91sec. Gay, though, was eliminated, having failed to recover from his hamstring injury; he finished fifth behind Powell. The world champion would not even contest the Olympic 100 metres final.

And when that final came, the starter's gun seemed to set alight 91,000 camera flashes around the Bird's Nest. It was Bolt in lane four who was propelled out of his blocks and on his way into history. Within two giant strides, Bolt was ahead, and the moment he started to drive, at around forty metres, a gap between him and the rest of the world's best sprinters started to open up, chasm-like in its rapidity. This was 'sprinting in excelsis' as one commentator called it.

No one ever got close to making a race of it. Powell, drawn out in lane seven, once again in a major final succumbed to his nerves. By sixty metres, Bolt could have slowed to a walk and still have claimed the gold. He was more flamboyant than that, though.

Bolt worked at his race for thirty-four strides, then, spotting himself on the giant screen at the top end of the stadium, he began arm-pumping and breast-beating, spread his arms wide and coasted across the line. He still crossed the finishing line in less time than anyone had ever run 100 metres before in history, including himself: 9.69 seconds.

Bolt's brilliance had stunned the rest. Richard Thompson, from Trinidad, finished two-tenths of a second behind – a massive margin at this level – and took the silver medal, while the bronze went to Walter Dix, of the United States, in 9.91sec. All three medallists ran personal bests. Powell, despite a better start than his younger teammate, finished only fifth.

'The fastest field that this planet can assemble had been treated not as competitors but as victims, their only purpose to make the champion seem swifter,' Patrick Collins wrote in the *Mail on Sunday* in Britain.

Bolt continued to speed around the track long after the finishing line, oblivious initially to his time, more caught up in the delight of being the Olympic champion. Down the back straight, he looked out for his mother and Norman Peart, who he knew had seats somewhere among the crowd there. When he saw his mother, he went over for a hug, Peart slapping his young charge on the back.

BOLT HAS NEVER had a good time with his racing shoes throughout his career. When preparing for his first global title, when teenaged nerves enveloped him in 2002, he nearly put his shoes on the wrong feet. Earlier in 2008, in New York before his first record run, Bolt noticed that one of his shoes was missing a spike – not a major difficulty, as he would later demonstrate, but a distraction, and hardly the sort of kit malfunction you would expect for someone with a multi-million dollar endorsement contract.

And on this night of nights in Beijing, Usain Bolt had managed to race 100 metres in just 9.69 seconds with his laces undone. With such winged feet, you begin to wonder whether Bolt really needs racing shoes at all.

Usain Bolt, the sprinter in excelsis from the island of sprinters, thus began a week for Jamaica and Jamaicans such as had never been seen before. Jamaican athletes would win eleven medals in Beijing, six of them gold – Bolt at the centre of three of them, fulfilling his destiny at 200 metres later in the week as he broke the twelve-year-old record set by Michael Johnson by running half a lap of the track in 19.30sec, an average of 23 miles per hour – the sort of speed that might get you a ticket in parts of London.

And in the 4x100 metres relay, Nesta Carter and Michael Frater set up Bolt for the third leg and he handed over to Asafa Powell who ran 8.7 and ended America's eight-year hold on another track world best.

Every Jamaican medallist hailed Bolt as their inspiration. Their successes – Shelly-Ann Fraser winning the women's 100 metres the night after Bolt's 100, Veronica Campbell-Brown taking gold in the 200 – were dubbed 'the Bolt effect'. The Prime Minister, Bruce Golding, telephoned to tell him that the streets of the capital were gridlocked with a national party going on. It was not long before Bolt was featuring on the Jamaican post office's postage stamps.

Bolt's celebrations, both before and after the race had finished, were not universally approved. His lightning bolt pose, which he says he struck spontaneously for the first time on the night of his 100 metres triumph, and the dance moves around the track during the lap of honour, brought complaints from Jacques Rogge, the President of the International Olympic Committee.

The Belgian surgeon had spent much of the previous decade trying to 'modernise' the Olympics, and make the Games more attractive to a younger audience. Rogge's criticism of Bolt seemed horribly out of step with a young man's sheer delight at what he had just managed to achieve.

'Usain is very humble off the track,' said Germaine Mason, the Jamaican-born British high jumper who had been a junior teammate of Bolt. 'He's not like what you see on the TV.

'I disagree with what Jacques Rogge said. When you win an Olympic medal that's the greatest thing ever, you don't just want to win and walk off the track, you want to entertain the crowd. You want to open up and express how you're feeling. His celebrations are a very good thing for the sport.'

In Jamaica, Bolt's celebrations were applauded. His dance moves put Jamaican popular culture on the map. Jamaican flag in one hand and his gold running spikes in the other, Bolt danced to the bafflement of the rest of the world. 'It's a thing in Jamaica. You wouldn't really understand,' Bolt said. 'I made it my celebration. My celebration to the world.'

Within a day, it seemed Rogge had been won round: Bolt was no longer just the future of athletics, he was now the future of the Olympic Games, too.

Chapter 4

How Does He Do It?

SOMETIMES, YOU WITNESS something, and you want to believe your eyes. And yet...

In the case of Usain Bolt and his achievements in Beijing, the simple facts raised so many questions, since they appeared to defy all known logic, of athletics history, of biomechanics. How could he run so much faster than so many convicted drugs cheats?

It was not just Bolt's 100 metres performances that raised questions. In the decade and more after Michael Johnson ran 19.32sec to win the 200 metres in record time at the Atlanta Olympics, no one had got within three-tenths of a second of that world record. Bolt managed to do it in his eighth race in less than a week. His Beijing 200-metre time knocked more than six-tenths from his own best time from the beginning of the season. In modern athletics terms, that represents a quantum leap in performance.

And here was a man who at the start of 2008 had never broken 10.00 seconds for 100 metres, yet who within eight months had knocked three-tenths off his own best time, and managed to win the Olympic final in 9.69 seconds. That is, a whole one-tenth of a second faster than when Ben Johnson broke the record, and broke the rules, in 1988.

That day in Seoul in September 1988 had scarred track and field for two decades, the image of Johnson, his finger pointing heavenwards as he celebrated before the line, his unfeasibly wide margin of victory over Carl Lewis, for ever etched on the memory as a symbol of how the sport had been corrupted.

Such was the scandal, even just in prospect, that to this day it is uncertain whether Johnson would have ever been unmasked as a drugs cheat had not a Korean lab technician leaked the essential details to a news agency, forcing the hand of the International Olympic Committee and track and field's world governing body. In the past quarter-century, it has always tended to be federal law-enforcers, whether with the Tour de France, the BALCO affair in America or Operation Puerto in Spain, rather than the sports authorities who have managed to expose the biggest doping scandals in sport.

It is worth stating that of the eight men who lined up for that infamous 100 metres final at the Seoul Olympics in 1988, seven were subsequently banned for drug use or had issues regarding doping control – including Lewis himself, who was forced to admit that he had three times failed tests, but that these adverse results were covered up ahead of the Seoul Games by the US Olympic Committee. The Briton who collected a silver medal following Johnson's disqualification, Linford Christie, was also 'given the benefit of the doubt' over his own adverse finding of stimulants at those 1988 Games. Years after he won the 100 metres gold medal in Barcelona in 1992, Christie's lengthy career was finally ended by a positive drug test.

Through the 1990s and into the 21st century, the litany of shame just kept getting longer. Justin Gatlin, the 2004 Olympic 100 metres 'winner', Dennis Mitchell, Marion Jones, Tim Montgomery, Kelli White: all won world or Olympics titles or broke records, and all were found to have been using banned drugs.

Those are just the ones who got caught. There are others around whom the whiff of suspicion proved to be very strong.

Just as notorious as Big Bad Ben at the Seoul Olympics was Florence Griffith-Joyner, who died having never convinced many of her peers that her stunning performances were not aided by illegal performance-enhancing drugs. Griffith-Joyner never tested positive for drugs, but after racing to times in Korea that seemed superhuman, suddenly in early 1989, she announced her retirement, never to run again. She died, sadly, in 1998, aged just 38. Her record of 10.49sec in the 100 metres has never been matched, not even by Marion Jones when she was at her steroid- and EPO-fuelled worst.

Maurice Greene was another who held the men's 100 metres world record. In 2000, in California, I visited him ahead of that year's Olympic Games in Sydney, where he would fulfil people's expectations and win the 100 metres gold medal. The previous summer, he had set the world best at 9.79 seconds, exactly the figures which Ben Johnson had recorded in Seoul.

'Don't you feel at all uncomfortable with that time, with the comparisons, because of the questions it might raise?' I asked. 'Wouldn't it have been easier for you had you run just one-hundredth quicker, just to avoid that time?'

'No,' Greene replied. 'Not at all. I'm happy with my time.' There was no hand of history tapping on Maurice Greene's shoulder.

Years later, having retired from competitive athletics after never failing a drugs test or ever being convicted of a drugs offence, Greene, who won five world championship gold medals as well as four Olympic medals, including gold in the 100 metres in Sydney in 2000, was involved in a court case in America in which it was alleged drug supplier Angel Heredia provided him with $10,000-worth of steroids.

Greene did not deny taking the goods from Heredia. He said he bought them for fellow athletes. 'Our group was very close and things always came up,' Greene said in evidence. 'I would pay for stuff and not care what it was. I've paid for things for other people.'

Heredia, it has to be said, is no angel, but you think he might have had a point when he he told the *Daily Mirror*, 'So Maurice says he paid the $10,000 for someone else? A guy said to me, "I want a friend like that." '

Welcome to the world of international athletics, where seeing is not always believing.

The authorities rarely make it any easier for athletes to demonstrate that they are 'clean', either, as they usually claim to be hidebound by protocol and confidentiality when it comes to producing details of drug tests taken. Thus, when a sportsman says that they are tested regularly and often, there's rarely an opportunity for anyone to verify what they claim.

This was the case at the Atlanta Olympics. Before 1996, it used to be said that the Irish swimming team was having a good Games if none of them drowned. Then, as if from nowhere, Michelle Smith, previously a modest international backstroke swimmer, plunged into the Olympic pool and scooped four gold medals.

Asked whether her relationship with Erik de Bruin, her boyfriend and coach, a drug-banned Dutch discus thrower who apparently could not even swim, might have had anything to do with her rapid improvement, Smith challenged any journalist to dare write a sentence linking her with the 'D' word. 'I'm the most tested swimmer in the history of the sport,' Smith said.

Except that she was not. Ireland, at that time, had no effective drug testing programme, so she was rarely, if ever, tested after racing at home, and certainly not out of competition, because when she returned the mandatory 'whereabouts' form to enable the drug testers to locate her, large swathes of the paperwork were left blank.

It took a new sports regime in Ireland, and a determined drug tester, to spring a surprise test on Smith one morning long after her triumphant return from Atlanta as a national heroine. After lengthy appeals and hearings, going all the way to the international Court for Arbitration in Sport in Switzerland, Smith was eventually found to have deliberately tampered with her urine sample by adding whiskey in an effort to render it impossible to test it.

Never found guilty of using drugs, the adulteration of her sample at the drug test was enough to see Smith banned for two years. She still has her Olympic medals, though.

It seems obvious now that Smith exploited the failings of the international drug testing system to her advantage, and even by 2011, eleven years after the founding of the World Anti-Doping Agency (WADA), there exists a situation where the controls on athletes in one country, or in one sport, can be a good deal stricter than those that apply in another jurisdiction.

So it was that even by 2007 there was no national anti-doping agency in Jamaica, and no out-of-competition testing programme such as those in the United States or Europe. Indeed, for the major meets in Jamaica in 2008 and 2009, testers had to be flown in by the world governing body.

Even by the end of the 20th century, most anti-doping campaigners had concluded that this kind of in-competition testing was a mere nicety, and almost a waste of time and money. Well-organised dopers would ensure that they were 'clear' of any trace of drugs before going to a competition and facing a likely mandatory test.

It is out-of-competition testing, especially in the off-season when athletes are undertaking their heaviest training workload, that is most effective in deterring drug use or catching the cheats, the experts say. 'You have to be stupid to be caught in an in-competition drug test,' the late Charlie Francis, notorious as the coach of Ben Johnson, once said.

You can only try to imagine, then, the reactions of officials at the IAAF's headquarters in Monte Carlo in June 2009 – just weeks before their World Championships were about to be staged in Berlin – when the news came through that their flying squad of testers who had attended the Jamaican championships in Kingston had come back with samples that contained traces of a banned drug.

Two of the sprinters involved, Yohan Blake and Marvin Anderson, were even part of the same Glen Mills training group as Usain Bolt.

Blake, Anderson, Allodin Fothergill and Lansford Spence all admitted that they tested positive for methylhexanamine, a stimulant usually found in nasal decongestant inhalers.

Nothing was said during the case to suggest that Mills or Bolt were involved.

The Jamaican disciplinary panel's initial ruling was that no offence had been committed because the substance was not explicitly mentioned on WADA's list of banned drugs. The ruling by the domestic Jamaican body risked the ire of the IAAF and WADA, but this was avoided when Jamaican officials reversed the decision on the grounds that the drug was a 'related substance' to products that were on the list.

Blake, for one, was withdrawn from the Jamaican relay squad for the Berlin championships, and told to serve a three-month ban from competition later in the year (when few Jamaican athletes would be competing in any case).

Two years later, amid a controversy of a different kind, and Blake was winning the 100 metres world title in Daegu.

And not much, according to one senior anti-doping official, had changed to improve drug testing in the Caribbean by 2011.

Travis Tygart is the chief executive of the US Anti-Doping Agency (USADA), a body launched in 2001 by lawyer and former Olympic marathon champion Frank Shorter, with help and finance from Congress, in a determined effort to take the administration of sports drug testing out of the hands of 'partial' bodies, including the US Olympic Committee and the national track and field federation.

In an interview with the London *Daily Mail* newspaper in August 2011, Tygart complained that drug testing in Jamaica, Spain and Russia was still not stringent enough and did not involve no-notice out-of-competition testing or tests for EPO and human growth hormone.

Two potential contenders for the 100 metres at the 2011 World Championships in Daegu, Mike Rodgers, from America, and Jamaica's Steve Mullings, were both withdrawn just days before the meeting following adverse drug test results. In the case of

Mullings, who had been part of the Jamaican relay team with Bolt that won world gold in 2009, it was the second positive test of his career, which risked a possible life ban.

'There does currently exist a divide between a number of nations that are running the most effective programmes,' Tygart said. 'You look at the UK, France, Norway and, hopefully, the US. They are in stark contrast to the quality of the programmes in Spain, Jamaica, Russia. That's troubling particularly because our athletes will be on the world stage competing against those athletes.

'Frankly, athletes from those countries deserve to be able to say: "Hey, we're clean. And not only are we clean but we're held to the highest standard." I feel bad for athletes from those countries, because they don't have the ability to say that,' Tygart said.

Such is the history and background that generates such cynicism in modern athletics.

Bolt, though, has never failed a drug test and, we are told, has been tested frequently. Ahead of the Beijing Games, we were told he had been tested 11 times that year, four times in the month before the Games. Increasingly, blood tests are being used in athletics, not just to try to detect banned substances, but to build up an 'athlete profile', to monitor any unusual or unexpected changes in the athlete's body chemistry. In Daegu in 2011, the IAAF paid for every competitor in every event to be blood tested.

'I've never done drugs, and I never will. I was tested four times before I even started running, urine and blood tests,' he said in Beijing. 'I've been tested so many times now I've lost track. I have no problem with that, we work hard and we're clean and any time they want to test us it's fine.'

ALL OF WHICH would bring many people back to a simple question about Bolt: how does he do it?

A few months after the Beijing Games, I asked that very question of Donovan Reid, Olympic 100 metres finalist in 1984 in Los Angeles, now a respected coach based in London. Reid had raced against Johnson, against Lewis and against Christie.

He offered a simple explanation for Bolt's speed. 'He's a freak of nature, simple as that,' Reid said. 'There's never been a sprinter of his height, with his stride length, and, most important, with his leg speed before. Everyone's always assumed that to be a great sprinter you need to be six-foot, six-foot-two max. Bolt's shown that's not the case.

'There's no knowing how quick he can go. Let's face it, it's not as if he is technically very polished, his start can be a bit iffy, and at 200 his bend running is poor. It's frightening to think what he just might do if he got all that sorted out, ran the perfect race, and didn't ease up at the finish to celebrate. But if he did that, he wouldn't be Usain Bolt, would he?'

Reid's coach's eye view of Bolt's build, running style and technique was a perspective that, over the coming months, appeared to be shared by others.

Marie-José Perec, the Frenchwoman who in 1992 and 1996 won three Olympic gold medals, two at 400 metres and one at 200, takes a similar view to Reid. Like Bolt, Perec was unusually tall compared to her rival sprinters. 'He is a force of nature,' she said of Bolt, 'a one-in-a-million runner.

'He has the advantages of a small man and a big man, with the explosiveness and stride frequency of a short runner and the stride length of a tall one.'

One man who has known Bolt for longer than most, Stephen Francis, Asafa Powell's coach, even thinks the question absurd. 'It's not explainable how they do what they do,' Francis said. 'It doesn't mean he's cheating, he's just using what he has. Usain ran 19.9 aged 17, when he was a skinny kid. Look at him now; 19.3 is not that surprising.

'I can't stop people doubting. People always have a way of belittling or trying to explain things they can't understand by saying, "Yeah, Usain Bolt, he's cheating, he's not real." But in the world people come along who are exceptional. You have Einstein, you have Isaac Newton, you have Beethoven – you have Usain Bolt.'

But there are others for whom questions remain. Bolt's predecessor as the last man to do the 100/200 metres double at an Olympic Games, Carl Lewis, has raised a perfectly groomed eyebrow at some of the performances.

'He could be the greatest sprinter of all time. I don't know. But I think it's interesting how in our sport, in our times, how someone can make that sort of dramatic change. For someone who ran 10 seconds and now they are talking they can run 9.4 seconds the next year, it just boggles the mind.

'I was in Osaka and I saw the 200 metres. I saw Tyson Gay just drill him and one year later

Bolt breaks the world record. That's a huge improvement in a year. And in the 100 metres it's gone from ten flat to nine point seven. It's a huge improvement.'

Just as the world governing body for athletics, the IAAF, saw Bolt as the superstar who could revive track and field's fortunes after years of scandal, so his own coach, Glen Mills, believes that his charge ought to be a role model.

'It's not going to be easy, but he can bring back respectability and credibility to sprinting,' Mills said in an interview in 2008. 'I can understand the cynics viewing with suspicion outstanding performances but from where I sit, I can't even get Usain to take natural vitamins.'

Mills is full of admiration for Bolt's abilities. 'Donkeys will never win the derby,' he said. 'He's the most talented athlete I've coached by far, with phenomenal raw top-end speed. Many have talent, but it's no good without competitiveness. The only one comparable I've coached is former world champ Kim Collins.'

Tyson Gay once described running in the lane alongside Bolt as 'feeling like you were going to get his knees in your face any minute', which is less of an exaggeration than you may think: Bolt's stride length is seven inches longer than Gay's. That means that Bolt uses just forty-one, sometimes forty-two strides, to cover the 100 metres. Most sprinters need forty-five.

'We actually reduced the length of his stride slightly,' Mills said, 'because he was over-striding, spending too much time in the air and not getting enough forward momentum.'

Inevitably, the coach also thought he could get Bolt to go faster still. Mills said he had worked to stop Bolt leaning in on the bend in the 200 metres, which had also helped his 100, while more strength work would also have an impact. 'The stronger he's now becoming, his stride frequency will improve and he'll run even faster,' Mills warned.

Once you have asked 'how could he do it?' the next question Bolt's performances inevitably prompted was 'just how fast can he go?'

For years when the 100 metres record has been broken it was usually in tiny increments: a hundredth of a second here or two-hundredths of a second there.

On October 14, 1968, Jim Hines ran 9.95sec in the Mexico City Olympics. But a generation before that, 10.2sec was considered to be a world-class time. Now, that performance probably would not get you into the semi-finals at the London Olympics.

There are several reasons why athletes have been getting faster and stronger. The shoes worn by today's sprinters are custom-made, featherweight, computer-designed marvels, a world away from the crude spiked shoes, often made of heavy leather, worn by top athletes a generation ago.

Running tracks are now firmer than ever before, with just the thinnest of rubber layers laid over a firm, tarmacadam-type structure. This is loved by the sprinters, who like the fast feel of the track, with less energy wasted.

Factor in modern, full-time training methods and improved diets for most people in the developed world from birth, and what we have been witnessing to some extent over the last fifty years of modern sport is an accelerated version of man's evolution.

There is another reason people are getting quicker: the growth in human population. Simply, with more people alive, the chances of a record being broken increase all the time as the pool of talent increases. And as time goes on, the chances increase of 'outliers', the 'freaks of nature" – which some suggest is the case with Bolt – who are simply in a different league to everyone else in their discipline.

In 2008, a specialist in animal locomotion at Stanford University in California, Mark Denny, published a study in *The Journal of Experimental Biology* in which he compared the running performance of humans with dogs and horses.

He found that speeds among the top racing greyhounds and equine thoroughbreds plateaued in the 1940s through to the 1970s, whereas human males continued to get faster, possibly as a simple result of population increase. Denny suggests that male sprint performance will level off at about 9.48 seconds – somewhere close to where Bolt himself has said he would like to run.

Might Bolt achieve that sort of performance at the London Olympics?

Certainly, it is possible according to scientists, but only provided that Bolt and Coach Mills have been working on the sprinter's stride length and power off the track, rather than the rate at which he turns his legs over.

Careful analysis of Bolt's record runs have shown that he broke the record by moving his legs at virtually the same pace as his competitors.

At the end of the 1990s, Peter Weyand, a professor at Southern Methodist University, conducted a study on speed. Comparing athletes to non-athletes, Weyand clocked both test groups as they ran at their top speed. What he found shocked him.

'The amount of time to pick up a leg and put it down is very similar,' he said. 'It surprised us when we first figured it out.'

Weyand discovered that speed is dependent upon two variables: the force with which one presses against the ground and how long one applies that force. In a full sprint, the average person applies about 500 to 600 pounds of force. An Olympic sprinter can apply more than 1,000 pounds.

But force isn't the only factor. How quickly that force is applied factors in as well. Weyand found that the average or untrained person's foot is on the ground for about 0.12 seconds per stride, while an Olympic sprinter's foot is on the ground for just 0.08 seconds.

'The amount of time your legs are in the air is 0.12sec, regardless if you're fast or slow,' Weyand said. 'An elite sprinter gets the aerial time they need with less time on the ground to generate that lift because they can hit harder.'

Dan Pfaff was the coach to Donovan Bailey, another Jamaican-born Olympic 100 metres champion.

Bailey won gold in Atlanta in 1996 running for Canada, to where his parents had emigrated when he was a child. By 2011, Pfaff was working with British athletics, based at the high-performance centre at Pickett's Lock in north London.

Pfaff suggests that Bolt's performances ought to have athletics coaches going back to first principles, and re-learning their physics. Speed is all about levers, and the longer the better, Pfaff says. 'If you're digging a hole in the ground, you have to get a longer lever to pry out a rock. If you can control those levers and make them work efficiently, it's a huge advantage.'

The momentum of Bolt's mass is another factor in his fantastic speed. While getting started and getting up to top speed may continue to be a problem for such a tall, and big, man, 'If you're that large, once you're moving, you stay moving,' according to Mike Young, an American strength and conditioning coach.

'He has the holy triumvirate,' Young said of Bolt. 'He's one of the top accelerators, he has the highest top-end speed and the highest endurance. It's something that's never been seen before.'

By the end of 2009, Bolt's impact on athletics had seen him transcend sport and become a cultural icon. The British magazine, the *New Statesman*, not usually known for being overly enamoured with sport, placed Bolt at fortieth in its list of fifty people who matter in the world today. After the death of Osama Bin Laden Bolt must have moved up at least one position since then.

The *New Statesman*'s summary of Bolt's importance to the world homed in on his peak performance: 'His tauntingly casual stride across the finishing line has become one of the resonant images of the 21st century: his yellow Jamaica vest alone at the front of the pack. He is now recognised as the most extraordinary athlete in the world, ever. His success, combined with his humour and popularity, has reignited the world of athletics and the Olympic Games, tainted in recent years by drug scandals.

'Bolt's performance signals the end of US dominance in track and field sports. But most of all, he has shown the peak of physical ability – a human being at the limit of his bodily powers.'

Chapter 5

Bolt, his BMW and Berlin

THE LATE CLIFF TEMPLE, the much respected former athletics correspondent of the *Sunday Times* and a successful coach to Olympic distance runners, used to have a saying about the transient nature of an athlete's career: 'They're always just a hamstring injury away from oblivion.'

In Usain Bolt's case, come April 29, 2009, oblivion for the triple Olympic champion almost came at the edge of a country road in Jamaica when the world's fastest man was showing off his new, top-of-the-range BMW M3 to two women passengers. Even he admitted afterwards that he was lucky to crawl from the wreckage still alive.

The six months following the Beijing Olympics had flown past in a swirl of awards dinners, in Jamaica and across the globe, plus various celebrity appearances, and almost more offers than Bolt's business managers could cope with. Had there been an entire relay team of Usain Bolts to share around, it would not have been enough to sate the public's appetite to meet, speak to or simply gawp at the sprinter.

At twenty-two years old, it's fair to say that Bolt was living the dream. Puma, his commercial backers ever since he had left school, were renegotiating their endorsement deal, with a £21 million, five-year arrangement which would lock in the globally recognised character right the way through the peak of his track career. As it was, industry experts estimated that Bolt's golden moments in Beijing had already netted him at least $400,000 in bonuses for winning the Olympic titles and setting the world records. At one of the more obligatory award ceremonies he attended, Bolt even received a cheque for $100,000 from the International Association of Athletics Federations as their 'Athlete of the Year', handed over in Monte Carlo by Prince Albert.

And the IAAF had good cause to be grateful. The remoulding, reshaping and redirecting of the sport internationally, all rebuilt around Bolt, was coming to fruition in a manner that they might have only imagined in the wildest of fantasy dreams. Now was the time for the next phase.

Someone in the office at Monte Carlo had been working on yet another relaunch of the series which connected the major Grand Prix meetings in Europe and around the world: what had been the Golden 4, then the Golden League, would soon become the Diamond League, where all events would be contested at each meeting, and the key athletes would have to meet in head-to-head competitions each week. At least, that was the theory. Backed with a multi-million sponsorship deal from an as yet-unnamed Asian electronics manufacturer, the faces of the Diamond League were to be Usain Bolt and the Russian pole vaulter, Yelena Isinbayeva.

Separate to this, Bolt's management's negotiations for race appearances in 2009 and beyond had seen the asking price for the Jamaican to step on a track soar towards six figures, in US dollars (the currency normally used on the track circuit). It meant that Bolt could expect to receive the equivalent of £6,000 per second for running in any 100 metres race. Promoters were happy to pay it, because a meeting with Bolt would ensure a sell-out crowd and was certain to satisfy their sponsors.

Bolt had transcended sport. They say that a person has reached 'iconic' status when they are known universally, in whatever language is spoken, from a *favela* in Rio de Janeiro, to Fifth Avenue in New York, to the banks of the Seine in Paris, to the Forbidden City in Beijing: Pele, Ali, Marilyn, Madonna. Now Bolt.

Suddenly, as if transformed in 9.69 seconds, athletics was fashionable again.

In 2003, during the World Championships staged in Paris, television viewing figures in Britain made headlines because of how many millions had switched off. In 2009, during the Berlin World Championships, BBC2 had peak figures of 5.2 million for Bolt's 100 metres final (on a Sunday evening) and 3.9 million for the 200 metres final (in midweek). People watch athletics now because of him.

Even the 'intelligentsia', who often in the past might sneer at anything so base as an activity which required a little perspiration was being turned on to athletics by Usain Bolt it seemed. The acclaimed English writer Margaret Drabble captured some of the wonder that this new audience was finding in watching Bolt race, even if it was by accident because of a late transmission of *Gardeners' World*:

'I've surprised myself by watching some of the athletics this summer. They are compulsive viewing. I found them by mistake, tuning in to *Gardeners' World*, which I watch in deference to my presenter son Joe Swift, but Joe had been postponed because of drama on the track.

'How nerve-racking and brutal are these live events, and how intrusive the interviewers! You have just come seventh in the 400 metres, way below your personal best, and there is some guy squatting in front of you, seconds later, nostril to nostril, eyeball to eyeball, asking how you feel about it. And you have to gulp back your manly tears and be brave. It is hideous.

'How we love competition, defeat, grief. I don't understand cricket, and can rejoice only by proxy that we won the Ashes, but even I could see Usain Bolt streak ahead. I may become addicted in time for 2012.'

You can almost imagine the marketers at the IAAF taking that passage and building entire commercial presentations around it, although BBC television's trackside interviewer, Phil Jones, might have squirmed just a little when he read it.

Usain Bolt was in such demand in the post-Olympic social whirl and partying in the autumn of 2008, that his coach, Glen Mills, even decided to let him take an extra three weeks off training, in addition to the regular end-of-season break. 'I was worn out,' Bolt said. It was something of a risk, in terms of preparing for the 2009 track season, which would culminate in the World Championships being staged in Berlin in August, but Mills calculated that a bigger risk would be to get Bolt back in training too soon and prompt some sort of injury or setback. Far better, in that laid-back, Jamaican way, they reasoned, to enjoy the moment.

'I really had to work hard for three or four weeks to catch up,' Bolt said later of his return to training at the end of 2008. 'There was hardly any social life for me, which was almost as painful as the training.'

But the transient nature of his fame, and fortune, was brought home to Bolt one afternoon in April, just as he was about to begin a new track season. He had just returned to Jamaica from Boston, where he had undertaken another appearance for Puma. He was driving along Highway 2000 outside St Catherine in his new car, a gift from grateful sponsors, after a brief tropical rainstorm, when the car left the road.

'I was going along sensibly,' Bolt stated in his biography. The car spun and flipped into the air after hitting the kerb, turning over three times before landing on its roof in a ditch.

Stunned and a little scared and shaken by the crash, Bolt got himself free from the car and then helped the two girls, one of whom had suffered a few bruises, while the other had taken a bang to the head and hurt her knee. Bolt had been driving barefoot, and while he managed to escape from the car relatively unhurt, as he walked round the car he trod on several thorns. When he was discharged from Spanish Town hospital later that day, his only bandaging was around his feet, where the surgeons had removed the thorns.

'I must be blessed,' Bolt was to say, 'because everyone in that car could have died. I've been very lucky.'

Such was the sprinter's new, elevated status within Jamaican society, Bolt's crash even prompted a statement in the Jamaican parliament. 'The reports that we have received is that he is not seriously injured and therefore Jamaica can collectively breathe a sigh of relief,' Andrew Holness, the leader of parliament, said in an adjournment motion, to thunderous applause from all political parties.

The leader of the opposition, Portia Simpson Miller, expressed her 'joy that nothing happened to Usain. We hope that they would be able to get over this kind of shock'.

The car was a write-off. And for someone with scoliosis, this was exactly the sort of accident Bolt really could have done without.

Once discharged from hospital, Bolt spent a couple of days undergoing further physio checks, while his sore feet had to be allowed to heal. He was unable to train for almost two weeks.

It was a bleak reminder of the gloomy period Bolt had endured when he turned pro. In one interview in 2010, he admitted that there were times when he had come close to giving up the sport altogether.

'There was a period between 2004 and 2007 when I was always injured,' Bolt said. 'Athletics was a torture for me. I had very short, but very painful, seasons. I've got a nasty scoliosis but, luckily, I started to treat it when I started training with Mills in 2007.

'If I'd continued as before, I would probably given up and stopped. Now I always do lots of exercises to strengthen the back muscles. I can't ever stop. Living without injury is important but you have to be very careful to avoid it; you need to keep on working hard.'

Speaking in a staged interview in front of a gathering of international journalists ahead of the European track season in 2010, Bolt was asked how fast he thought he could run. Somewhat ludicrously, the cheerleader conducting the interview seriously suggested that, having recently clocked 8.7sec from a flying start at the Penn Relays, Bolt might think a sub-9.00sec time in a regular 100 metres would be possible.

Bolt, for his part, was polite, but very reasonable in his answer. 'Let's keep our feet on the ground,' he told his Italian questioner. 'Such a time isn't humanly possible.

'I'm always asked how fast man can go and I always say that 9.4sec could be the limit. Obviously, I make a judgement on my abilities but there could be another athlete able to do better in ten years' time.'

The questioner then put to Bolt his 400 metres potential, based on his having run one relay leg in 43.58sec. 'I didn't have time to realise that I was going towards martyrdom,' Bolt said of that experience.

'The fatigue I felt afterwards told me. No, the 400s are just training. I'm not even thinking about lengthening the effort for the time being.'

Bolt also dismissed fanciful suggestions that he could compete in a head-to-head against the great Ethiopian distance runner, Kenenisa Bekele, another double gold medal-winner at the Beijing Olympics, but at 5000 and 10,000 metres, the opposite end of the distance spectrum for track races.

Interviewing some athletes, whether through the formalised and often stilted mandatory post-event press conferences, or in the rough and tumble of a stadium's Mixed Zone, is rarely a satisfactory arrangement.

The Mixed Zone normally offers little more than a hurried, snatched word, which can be sent around the world by the news agencies and used to support a tabloid news line, but provides little true insight – the athlete is usually still out of breath after their competition, they might have a gash from a spike wound down their shin that requires prompt treatment if they have been in a particularly roughhouse middle-distance race, and they are always far more concerned about getting reunited with their kit, their coach and the bus back to their hotel or the Village than providing any immediate analysis of the race or opening up with their inner-most thoughts.

The no-holds-barred Mixed Zone, though, at least in theory affords journalists a form of direct access to the athletes of their choice. The rule is that athletes are supposed to stop at various points in the Mixed Zone, where they are forced to run the gauntlet through an established media 'pecking order'.

First, there's right-holder television interviews (for the broadcasters who have paid to cover the meeting; these are those who raised Margaret Drabble's ire), where someone like Bolt might be expected to stop for British, American, French and Spanish stations, as well as Jamaican TV; then there's non-rights-holding broadcasters (the TV and radio stations who might only be allowed to use clips from the event in their news bulletins); and then finally, the poor bloody infantry of the written press.

By the time most athletes reach the written press, they have probably already endured at least ten minutes of inane questions, so the newspaper, agencies and website reporters who inhabit the fag-end of the Mixed Zone often get short shrift from tired and bored athletes.

The fallback as far as medal-winners at major championships are concerned is often the formal press conference, which is staged as soon as possible, depending on the timing of the event and the schedule for the medal ceremonies. Because of the Tower of Babel nature of these press conferences, even when the medallists are all gathered together and relatively composed, the outcome for the journalist seeking real insight is rarely much better.

Normally this occasion is 'compered' by a local official who speaks English in an odd *mitteleuropean* inflection, with translators on hand for one or more of the medallists. The MC asks each competitor the same, suitably polite question, with the answers being delivered sometimes in two translated languages. The first twenty minutes of the half-hour slot might be taken up with just two 'non-question' questions in this manner and the almost deferential question almost always ignores the main news line which anyone who had just seen the event outside will want to know about.

And when the compere opens the press conference up to questions from the floor, that's when you get some real humdingers of simply stupid questions. This may not always be the journalists' fault: someone on a news desk, or the features desk in their office back in Madrid, or Brussels or, yes, London, clearly came up with a 'bright' idea at morning conference. This in turn has been relayed via the sports desk, and the reporter tasked with making sure he or she gets an answer. Puerile does not even start to describe some of the questions I've heard aired at such press conferences.

'Usain, what's your favourite colour?'

'Mr Bolt, what's your favourite food other than chicken nuggets?'

'Usain, you play golf. Do you think you could beat Tiger Woods?'

'What advice would you give a tourist coming to London?'

'Usain, how fast do you think you could go if you ran on your hands?'

All right, one of those might be made up. But only one. And the answer to the fourth question was 'An umbrella'.

Athletes, particularly the established and experienced ones who have endured this process before, have long ago wised up to their role in this game. Schooled by their team management, and their sponsors, through what is called 'media training' – basic premise: smile politely, answer all questions as banally as possible, say as little as possible – the question/answer combination rarely adds to the sum of human knowledge.

This, you may not be surprised to hear, is not usually the case at Bolt press conferences. But we shall return to that topic soon enough.

Despite a decade at the top of international distance running and strenuous efforts by his Dutch managers to make him more 'marketable' to the English-speaking audience (specifically America), Kenenisa Bekele still tends to use a translator at such press conferences.

Doubts have existed for a while about how truly verbatim the English translations of Bekele's responses might be. On one occasion, the runner must have spoken in response to a question for almost two minutes. His translator dutifully took down some notes, and when the athlete stopped speaking, they took the microphone and interpreted his response as: 'No.'

So the idea of putting an abstract concept to Bekele in a question at such a press conference ought really to be a non-starter. But after Beijing, one game journalist did dare, suggesting the ridiculous proposition of some sort of 'middle ground' race against Bolt.

Bekele's response was reported as, 'Oh, I would definitely beat him.'

What has remained unclear to this day was whether Bekele was talking about a race over 100 metres, 10,000 metres, or somewhere in the middle. Given Bolt's physical repulsion at the prospect of racing even a single lap of an athletics track, the very notion of the question ought to have been dismissed as the irrelevance that it is. Yet in the months afterwards, and armed with Bekele's 'answer', the prospect of such a head-to-head was raised again and again with Bolt.

This included the occasion of the international press conference in 2009, hosted by the senior Italian journalist. 'I won't even do 600 metres against Bekele,' Bolt said, to the surprise of no one who had listened to and understood his previous answers. 'A distance like that is a marathon for me.'

Bolt has raced as far as 300 metres on the European circuit. There are a number of reasons. For the promoter, it is the chance to bill Bolt's appearance as a 'record attempt', at a rarely run distance, where the achievement actually proves very little. For Bolt, the meaninglessness of the distance ensures that he has no great reputation at stake. Plus, it is an excellent training exercise, for which he is also paid handsomely.

Despite his many protestations about hating running hard over longer distances, Bolt's training sessions in Jamaica during the winter months will include repetition runs of 300, 400, 500 and even 600 metres. In the summer of 2009, when training on the Brunel University track in west London, Bolt even trained with a specialist 400 metres runner, old friend Jermaine Gonzales, running eight 150s, each completed in about 17sec, with just one minute's rest between efforts.

Sprinting, after all, is about much more than the ten seconds of effort we get to see on the telly: at championships, if Bolt is entered for the 100 and 200 metres, he'll routinely be expected to race seven or even eight times in less than a week, plus a relay, too. So such training sessions are necessary for world-class sprinters, as they build strength and some stamina that they hope to be able to call upon in the final twenty or thirty metres of their 100- and 200-metre races in the track season.

'It's easy to express yourself in the 300 metres,' Bolt has explained, 'because, after 200, you can go on inertia without getting to asphyxia. The extra 100 metres to get to 400 are lethal.'

Now, you might think that the line of questioning to the greatest 100 and 200 metres runner the world has ever seen about his racing other distances had been exhausted.

Oh no. Our compere then asked Usain Bolt, in all seriousness, whether he got bored racing just 100 and 200s.

'Why?' Bolt replied, apparently with the patience of a saint. 'I'd like to succeed in being the No. 1 sprinter for five or six years and so become a legend.'

When not training, enduring interviews or attending presentation dinners, Bolt's new found fame allowed him to start undertaking some charity and social work. Back at his parents' village at Sherwood Content in Jamaica, he put up the money to refurbish the local medical clinic and the primary school, where he had been born and educated. 'I think it's a duty to help my people,' he said. 'I realise that being a model for boys and girls and others it's right that I do it, because I've been lucky and it's a pleasure helping others.'

In Kingston, Bolt had started to invest some of his winnings in a business, too. 'I'm thinking about my future, when my career ends,' he said. 'I'll still be in sport, athletics, but I've also got other ideas.

'After opening Tracks & Records, the sports bar, I'm also thinking about a series of restaurants. I'd like to take the pleasures of Jamaican cooking into the world.'

By now, Bolt had found himself on a media treadmill. His waking hours became interwoven between his training sessions and races, essential for maintaining his USP, – 'unique selling point', as the marketing people like to call it – while also fulfilling the requirements of the sponsors who were paying him many millions of dollars.

So up to 2010, there would be some one-on-one interviews arranged with hand-picked reporters whose newspapers guaranteed a 'good show' for any resulting article, and whose questions would be pointedly directed at the latest clothing brand or product which Bolt had in some way endorsed.

So Bolt would not be asked about his race plans for the coming season, or his rivalry with Tyson Gay, or his relationship with Asafa Powell or his coach, Glen Mills. The interviews would elicit more 'human interest' answers, such as why he no longer wears a crucifix around his neck.

'Wearing jewellery made me lose races,' Bolt told the *Mail on Sunday*. 'I'm not into male jewellery any more. I used to wear a neck chain even when I competed, and I felt it used to impede me. In those days I used to lose a lot more than I do now, and my training staff said it was partly down to the chain – so it had to go.'

Then he might be asked about his wardrobe. 'I possess three nice suits and one truly horrendous one. I'm most comfortable in jeans and T-shirts, but every so often I need and like to wear a suit.

'I have three Hugo Boss suits – two black and a dark blue. But I also have a green suit that I bought when I was young. I used to really like it, but now I've outgrown it, which is just as well, because the truth is it's horrible..

'No man should ever wear pink. That's a terrible colour. The closest I've ever got to that was when a sponsor asked me to wear a shirt with yellow reflectors. It was for a photo shoot, and even as I was putting it on I was thinking, "Oh my God, what am I doing?" Everyone else was blinking as the light shone off the reflectors and into their eyes.

'The most expensive item of clothing I've ever bought I've worn just twice. I bought an Ed Hardy shirt in London the other year for £300. Nice as it is, spending that much money definitely wasn't worth it. It's not the sort of thing I usually do. I've only managed to wear it twice and I doubt I'll put it on again.

'I wear jeans to destruction. I love my black straight jeans so much – they're my favourite item.

I wear them to the point of them falling apart, and then I'll get a new pair. If you bump into me on a night out in Kingston, you'll see me in those jeans and a black T-shirt. I guarantee you!

'Where I live it's just too hot to put on a fashion show. During the day it's too hot to make much of an effort with clothes, so it's either my running gear or simple T-shirts and light shorts, just like everyone else in Jamaica. There's nothing fancy about me.

'I'd hate to have to dress like a golfer. I like to think I'd look OK in most outfits, but even I would shy away from full-on golf gear. You know what I'm talking about – the polo shirts are OK, but I'm not sure about the stuffy old shorts. As for the knee-length socks... please, don't they know how ridiculous they look?'

And so on. The modern-day obsession with celebrity requires that a sports star, someone known for their excellence as a track and field sprinter, must answer questions seeking to know whether they use any gentlemen's grooming products (he doesn't, in case you were wondering).

And all to secure a half-page ad in the same section of the newspaper.

For that first 18 months or so after Beijing, Bolt did seem to take everything very much in his stride. 'My motto is "keep it simple, keep it chilled". I'm a Jamaican, I'm laid-back and I don't get hung up about too many things in life. What you see is what you get.'

And in one interview, arranged by Puma with the *Mail on Sunday* to coincide with the launch of a clothing range, the sprinter did venture into areas closer to the track, and much closer to home.

'The biggest motivator in the world is the fear of losing,' Bolt said.

'I don't want to lose; I'm very competitive. My greatest fear as a professional athlete – in fact, the only fear I've ever had when racing – is the fear of losing. It's always there, and the only way you get over it is by focusing and by working harder and training harder than anyone else.'

Going into the 2009 track season, crawling from the wreckage of his written-off BMW, Bolt, as the triple Olympic champion from Beijing, had a great deal to lose.

Perhaps because of the reduced and interrupted pre-season training, and the car crash, Bolt had a very low-key track season in the summer of 2009. In May, despite still suffering some pain from the thorn wounds in his feet, Bolt turned out in Manchester, England, and ran a 150-metre straight street race, his time, 14.35sec, qualifying for another world record plaque.

In June, he duly turned up for, and won, his national titles in Kingston, securing his place on the Jamaican team for the Berlin World Championships at 100 and 200 metres.

The focus of attention then shifted to Europe, and the Grand Prix circuit, where Bolt and Tyson Gay, the defending world champion at 100 and 200 metres, fought a sort of 'phoney war', racing by proxy by never actually getting on a track together in the same race: Gay sped to 9.77sec in a 100 metres race in Rome; Bolt clocked 9.79sec in Paris.

I have been reporting on the IAAF's World Championships in one form or another since the very first, in Helsinki in 1983, and the 2009 event would see me attend my eighth successive edition of the event. Because of the venue, the grandly impressive Berlin Olympiastadion designed by Werner March in the 1930s to help glorify the Nazi regime of Adolf Hitler, there seemed to be a special poignancy about the 2009 World Championships, for Berlin, for Germany, and also for the sprinters.

The stadium has been updated many times since it staged the 1936 Olympics, where Hitler distorted and perverted the Olympic sports movement for his own propaganda. Most recently, the stadium had been overhauled thoroughly for the 2006 football World Cup, when Berlin, once again the capital of a re-united Germany, had staged the final.

But if you strolled around the buildings to study the history and the architecture, the evidence was still there; the odd swastika built into a carved marble statute here, a bronze plate with quasi-imperial pretensions there; wisely, the Berliners had not tried to eradicate the architecture in the mistaken belief that it would erase some of history's darkest moments. Better that it remains, to remind us.

As someone whose first visit to Berlin had been to the eastern half of a divided city, the experience of working at a championships in the modernised, unified Berlin was also novel, and a little exciting.

And what was particularly redolent for sprinters, such as Bolt, Gay and Asafa Powell, was the sporting legend that surrounds those 1936 Olympics, and the achievements of the black American sprinter, Jesse Owens. Anyone competing in the 100 or 200 metres on the Berlin track that week would be running in the footsteps of Owens, in the footsteps of greatness.

Gay and his American teammates all had the initials 'JO' on their US team vests for the championships, with special permission from the IAAF and in a clever marketing move by their sponsors, Nike, to lay some claim to an association with Owens which never actually existed.

Bolt did not get overly involved in the Owens' associations. Perhaps he was mindful of that part of the Jesse Owens story that is rarely told, of how the American sporting hero encountered just as much racism when he returned home to America as when he was racing in Hitler's Germany. The legend has it (not entirely correctly) that it was the German Fuhrer who snubbed Owens at a medal ceremony, when in fact the real snub came from Owens's own President, Franklin D Roosevelt, who failed to invite the four-time gold medallist to a reception at the White House.

While Owens may have given sporting history's most resonant performance, he returned to poverty, forced to use his sporting talent in stunt events, competing in undignified challenge sprints with racehorses.

THE DAY BEFORE the 2009 Berlin championships began, Bolt did turn out for an event where he was presented with a slab from the Berlin Wall, perhaps symbolic for the way he had managed to break down barriers, his German-based sponsors revelling in the success of their T-shirt sales in Jamaican black, gold and green to the usually proudly nationalistic German public.

As you travelled around the city either on the U-Bahn or on foot in the days before the championships, it was clear that this was to be Berlin's Bolt Show, and Gay and Powell and anyone else had mere walk-on parts.

Even at the formal, official press conferences Bolt attended, there was only ever one focus of attention. Bolt lapped it up, standing behind the table on the stage, pulling shapes, like his now 'trademark' Lightning Bolt pose, grinning, gurning and joking throughout the procedure, while the other athletes in attendance tried to deal with the media demands in their conventional manner.

'I just can't wait to get on the track,' he told his audience at a venue on Berlin's eastern side which had been done out, Caribbean style, as the 'Yaam Club'. 'I have no problems, I'm in really good shape. I'm just itching to run. I can't wait. You never know what's possible. I just want to run. I just want to go out there.'

Having been denied the opportunity to race against Gay in a championship final since he lost to the American in the 200 metres in 2007, Bolt chose to use this occasion for some typical sporting kidology. 'I'm looking forward to the showdown with Tyson Gay. It's a race, a competition, but it's not a fight. I don't take it personally; it's all business for me. So I'm going out there to just compete.

'I don't really put pressure on myself. I go out there and just take it one step at a time over the four rounds. And when it comes to the finals I just do what I have to do. Because I'm always ready to compete at my best.'

The Berlin championships, said Bolt, 'are very important because I haven't won World Championships gold. I set a standard for myself and I have to live up to it.'

He also sought to disarm questioners who ascribed arrogance to his pre-race antics. 'You have to be confident,' Bolt said. 'But I'm not too confident. I have confidence in my ability because I train hard. And I know I put the work in. So I'm confident in going out there and doing my best.

'I'm not unbeatable. I've said from the beginning of the season that someone can come and beat me on the day. But I'm not worried. I'm ready.'

And having dismissed the allegations of arrogance, Bolt's relaxed approach to racing, and races, seemed to be rubbing off on other sprinters, too. In the past, the 100 metres had always been built up as some form of heavyweight confrontation, like a boxing match without the punching. Big, strong sprinters, their shoulders and thighs bulging with power, would prowl around their starting blocks, grim-faced, staring down the straight, concrete-hard in concentration.

Not Bolt. Even at the World Championships he would step forward when the stadium public address announced his name; he'd grin broadly, pull another face, and gesture something or other with his hands.

Now, some of the other sprinters were adopting Bolt's approach, each trying to offer a pose or gesture of their own; even Bolt's Jamaican teammate, Asafa Powell, started to join in.

The sprinting career of Powell, four years Bolt's senior, had been painful to watch. Electric-fast all summer at the Grand Prix meets, breaking record after record, but come the championship event at the climax of the summer and Powell would somehow crumble, the pressure proving just too much for him. By 2009, Powell's five-year international career had yielded him four world records and yet only a solitary individual bronze medal from a possible five World Championships or Olympic Games.

Powell had become the living embodiment of any sprint coach's message: 'You can't run when you're tight.' In Berlin, Powell seemed to start taking that on board, loosening up. Powell no longer had the pressure of the title as 'world record-holder' weighing down on his shoulders, and with almost all the attention now on Bolt, even he allowed himself a smile and a wave before the 100 metres qualifying rounds in Berlin.

Yet all 86,000 people in the Olympiastadion – Bolt's presence ensured sell-out crowds even for the sessions with just qualifying rounds – sensed that once their favourite settled into his starting blocks for his first-round heat of the 100 metres at around lunchtime on Saturday, August 15, the opening day of the championships, he meant business.

As ever, the first round was a matter of routine for the likes of Bolt, Gay and Powell. The quarter-finals that evening also proved to be less than demanding, at least for Bolt, who, drawn alongside his training partner Daniel Bailey, treated the run as another training outing. With the best starts in the field, the pair, running stride-for-stride through the finish, shared glances and smiles, with Bailey getting being given the race win in 10.02 to Bolt's 10.03.

In the third quarter-final, Powell pulled away from Darvis Patton and managed to clock 9.95sec, despite easing up short of the line, the first sub-10sec performance of the competition. In his quarter-final, Gay looked like he had to work hard for his 9.98sec, one-tenth of a second ahead of another Jamaican, Michael Frater.

Business done, Bolt strode through the Mixed Zone – no obligations to talk to the press in between qualifying rounds – and back to his hotel. Sunday was finals day, with two races and a job to be done.

Yet Bolt very nearly did not even make it into the final. As is usual, the 100 metres semi-finals were staged early in the evening session, to give the qualifiers a couple of hours to recover and relax before the final showdown. But, just like national selection trials, even Usain Bolt has to ensure that he qualifies for the final.

Bolt had bet with Bailey on who could get the fastest reaction time – the official timing devices have pads fitted in all the starting blocks which measure when the athlete's foot presses and releases. Any reaction quicker than 0.10sec is regarded as anticipating the starter's gun; it triggers a signal to the race starter, and he or she sounds a recall for a false start.

Bolt did just that in his Berlin semi-final. 'I popped the blocks a fraction too early, and you could hear the shock and the 'ooohs' all round the stadium,' he would recall later. Under the false start rules as they stand in 2011 – as we shall see – that first false start would have led to Bolt's immediate disqualification. But in 2009, the first start error received just a warning.

When the starter called the sprinters forward a second time, again there was a false start: could it possibly have been Bolt again?

The pause while waiting for an official to issue the warning card seemed to last an age: eventually, the starter's assistant proffered a red card to Tyrone Edgar, a young British sprinter. Regardless of who had committed the first false start, under the rule as it stood then, whoever committed a subsequent false start would be automatically disqualified.

For a third time, the starter called the now seven sprinters to their blocks. And this time they got away smoothly enough. Bolt clocked 9.89sec. False starts permitting, he looked to be in outstanding form for the final a couple of hours later. He would need to be: in the other semi-final Gay won in 9.93sec. The American was not going to relinquish his world title without a battle.

What happened over the next 120 minutes or so – and the following week – there can now be little doubt, really got to Tyson Gay. It is not just what Bolt manages to do out in public, on the racing track, which manages to defeat his opposition, but also on the warm-up track and in the 'ready room' under the stadium, where the athletes have to wait just before they are called for their event.

Bolt remembers that night chatting and even dancing with his mate, Daniel Bailey, to while away some of the time. 'Tyson was looking at us as if to say, "What are they doing?"'

And while Bolt, Bailey and even Powell mugged for the TV cameras as they lined up for the race, Gay just got sterner, barely managing a wave to the crowd.

Into their blocks and the fun was over for everyone.

There were no false starts this time, and in 41 strides conducted amid a noise from the German crowd that sounded close to a sonic boom, Bolt produced what has to be regarded as the most perfect 100 metres race ever run.

Even the usually staid, conventional official report from the world governing body described the 100 metres final in Berlin as 'a performance that defies the imagination'.

Bolt had broken his own world record, running 9.58sec, knocking 0.11sec from the time he had run exactly a year ago to the day in Beijing. Witnesses to that 9.69sec run a year before had questioned how it was possible for Bolt to run so fast. Now Bolt had gone even faster, taking the largest chunk of time off the 100 metres world record since the introduction of fully electronic timing forty years before.

'I was definitely ready for the world record and I did it,' Bolt said. 'I didn't think I could run 0.1sec faster than my world record, but for me, anything is possible.

'I told you I would come here and do my best and I just did that. I did well, I feel good and I'm proud of myself.' Perhaps mindful of some of the questions that had been asked, particularly after the drug test scandal at the Jamaican championships earlier that summer, Bolt added: 'It's a great time but I can believe what I have achieved.'

GAY HAD GONE into the race knowing he had to be in front of Bolt after the first thirty metres. He never got the chance. Bolt got the jump on Gay, edging ahead of the American within those first two, explosive strides. Bolt dared not look to one side or the other, lest it cost him a fraction of time and the race. The Jamaican could sense, all the way down the straight, that Gay was close by, but at no point could he see the American.

In fact, Gay was timed at 9.71sec, the third-fastest 100 metres anyone had ever run and an American record. Yet he had been thoroughly beaten. Demolished as thoroughly as the Berlin Wall had been twenty years earlier.

Under the headline 'Insane! Usain!' the British tabloid the *Daily Mirror* reported the following day: 'Bolt's time of 9.58sec stopped the world in its tracks. Everybody who saw it gasped. Nobody will forget where they were on August 16, 2009.'

'I'm disappointed to have lost the race,' Gay said when a microphone was thrust in his direction, and he could make himself heard over the crowd, as Bolt lapped up his lap of honour, posing for pictures for the crowd, dancing around the cobalt blue track with Berlino the Bear, the championships mascot.

'But I ran my fastest time,' Gay said, almost as if entering a plea in mitigation. 'I just wanted to give my best. It wasn't enough but I'm happy to have the national record.'

The race may have also come close to answering one of the ultimate questions of the previous year: just how fast could Usain Bolt run 100 metres? For this time there was no showboating, no chest beating, as he ran hard to the line. Gay's racing had ensured that he needed to do so.

It is usually wrong to ascribe to any sportsman the idea that they perform to a certain level because of the offer of a cash prize on the line. Competition is usually the key: Bolt says that in training, the best he might ever manage is 10.7sec for 100 metres.

But put him in a race, and there's always the chance that a record-shattering performance might be summoned up. On this occasion, it delivered him another cheque for $100,000 from the championship organisers, plus whatever bonuses his agent had managed to negotiate with his sponsors.

The new, relaxed Asafa Powell took bronze for the second consecutive championships, running 9.84sec – only the fifteenth-fastest performance of his career. But for once, even in defeat, Powell appeared content. 'I'm so excited about Usain's run tonight, it is great to be part of this,' he said. 'Usain showed us that it is possible.'

Bolt's friend Bailey, after looking like a possible medallist in qualifying, placed fourth in the final, though in the inter-island Caribbean rivalry he at least got ahead of Richard Thompson, Trinidad's Olympic silver medal-winner from Beijing. Seven men in the final ran 10.00sec or faster.

By repute – and there is no evidence to prove this one way or another – after he crossed the finishing line in the Olympiastadion and galloped through his post-race media duties, Bolt then raced into central Berlin, where he embarked on an all-night party the likes of which only twenty-something Jamaicans are able to sustain. The rumour, again entirely unconfirmed, is that he did not return to his hotel bedroom until the Tuesday morning, almost 36 hours after the race.

There is nothing in Bolt's own statements or books since then to clarify whether this Berlin bender actually took place. Indeed, Bolt's own 2010 biography is notably absent of any commentary on how he might have celebrated such an achievement. Thus, it may be just the stuff of sporting legend. But it is fair to say that when he next re-appeared on the track, for the 200 metres heats, he did look like he needed a good night's sleep.

Tyson Gay needed more than simple bed rest. Was he in shock after the 100 metres final? By the Monday evening, ahead of the 200 metres first-round heats the following day, the American team had announced on the defending champion's behalf that a groin strain would prevent him from contesting the event, in the hope that he might be fit in time for relay duty at the weekend.

Apparently, Gay had been competing with the injury all season, even when clocking the 9.71sec. 'Rather than risk further injury, I've decided that I will not compete in tomorrow's first round of the 200 metres,' Gay was quoted in the statement as saying. 'I would like to be a part of Team USA's 4x100 metres and believe this decision will give me the best chance to be ready for the relay. I want to help our relay as best I can.'

IT WOULD BE unfair on the other world-class athletes entered for the Berlin 200 metres to say that this left the way open for Bolt. But it did.

It meant that while he may have looked a little sluggish and weary in the first two rounds, when he even took to wearing a team T-shirt under his canary yellow Jamaica racing vest, the only run that really mattered would be the final on the evening of Thursday, August 20, the night before Bolt's 23rd birthday.

A year earlier, at the end of a long week in which he extended the bounds of human achievement, Bolt had raced the 200 metres into a headwind of nearly 1 metre per second. In more favourable conditions, and now with the added confidence of having run the 100 metres even faster, what might be possible?

As the eight finalists got into their blocks, another packed audience was hushed for a moment. The Frenchman, David Alerte, broke the tension with an over-eager start. Bolt was slow to react. Was he still sluggish from his exertions earlier in the week?

Once the starter's gun fired again, we had our answer: possibly the best start Bolt had ever produced. As the staggered starting positions in the lanes on the bend evened out as the runners hit the home straight, Bolt was already four, five, six metres clear, and racing away from the best the world could assemble.

There was no question that he would win. The only matter to be resolved was how quickly: the clock stopped at 19.20 seconds. In the tumult and clamour, it took the German officials a couple of minutes before they were able to announce, after studying the photo-finish, that Bolt's time was rounded down to 19.19sec; again an improvement on his own, year-old world record of more than one-tenth, putting him 0.13sec faster than anybody else has ever managed. His winning margin – 0.62sec – was also a record, of sorts, as the largest seen in this event at the World Championships.

The clock watchers, biomechanists and other scientists videoing the performance reckoned that Bolt may have touched a top speed of 24mph during the race. And all this was achieved when running into a headwind once again (albeit a more modest 0.3m/s on this occasion).

Behind Bolt, Panama's Alonso Edward had hunted down the faster starting Shawn Crawford to snatch the silver, setting a world best for a 19-year-old of 19.81sec (faster than Bolt had run at the same age), with Wallace Spearmon third for the second successive World Championships in 19.85. Afterwards, Spearmon said that the experience of racing behind Bolt was so other-worldly, it was like being part of a video game.

Crawford crossed the line bitterly disappointed in fourth. It was the first time that four men had run faster than 19.90sec in the same race. It was also the first time in which five men had broken 20 seconds in one race.

For Bolt, it was another $160,000 pay day, with another world record bonus on top of his $60,000 first-place prize money. If he had been paid in plaudits, he could have added a zero or two to the end of those figures. One British newspaper described him as 'easily the biggest storm to emerge from the Caribbean since Hurricane Georges, the most substantial international star Jamaica has seen since Bob Marley'.

And the morning after his 200 metres win in Berlin, Bolt celebrated his birthday with breakfast in bed at his Berlin hotel. Even Usain Bolt, it seems, cannot keep up with Usain Bolt all the time.

Chapter 6

False Start

DAEGU PURPORTS TO be South Korea's third city, on a par, for instance, with Liverpool in England. There have not been any plans announced yet for Merseyside to stage the athletics World Championships, the world's third largest international sports event, after the Olympic Games and the football World Cup. Then again, Samsung, the electronics giant which has been bankrolling the IAAF since the middle of the first decade of this century, does not have a major operations base in Liverpool.

That is how it came about that Daegu was chosen to host the 2011 IAAF World Championships, and would be the place where for the first time Usain Bolt would arrive as a senior athlete with titles to defend. Three of them: the 100 and 200 metres and the 4x100 metres relay title he had won with his Jamaican team mates in Berlin.

The 100/200 metres double in Berlin had drained him, Bolt admitted, and come the relay final he felt that he contributed little more than just getting the baton round safely, with Asafa Powell running the anchor, or glory, leg. 'I was shattered,' Bolt said, 'far more than in Beijing.'

The end of the 2009 championships also presented Bolt with other problems, too, such as how to get his 'piece' of the Berlin Wall home. Not unreasonably, Bolt had expected to be presented with a tourist-sized lump. Instead, when he met the Berlin mayor, he had indicated to Bolt a 12-foot-high chunk of concrete with a less-than-flattering portrait of the runner in mural form on it. 'At least I think it was me,' Bolt said. 'The clue was that the figure was black and in a Jamaican running vest, but apart from that it could have been anyone.'

The piece of wall, weighing two tons, was eventually shipped to Jamaica, but Bolt so disliked the mural that he could not even have it in the garden of his new house. It now sits, unwanted and forlorn, in an army camp.

One other, far more useful souvenir was a £200,000, eight-lane blue running track, just like the one in the Olympiastadion, which a sponsor 'donated' to Bolt, and which he had installed at the Kingston university where he trains.

Inevitably, the meetings in Europe after Berlin, in the month or so before the end of the summer of 2009, were all a bit 'after the Lord Mayor's Show'. Bolt and the other top athletes had been living off adrenalin for the nine days of the World Championships. Getting themselves up again for competition afterward was a difficult task.

It certainly showed in Bolt's races, where he was nearly beaten over 100 metres in Zurich by Asafa Powell, and then finished off with a decent, if unspectacular, 200 metres in Brussels.

Bolt had originally been booked to race 100 metres at Brussels' Ivo van Damme Memorial by its long-time director, Wilfried Meert, a former sports journalist. Meert, experienced, always polite and someone who knows his sport inside out, had months earlier signed both Bolt and Tyson Gay to race one another at 100 metres. In the end, the match-up failed to materialise. Such is the nature of modern-day, professional athletics.

By now, with the three world titles to go with his three Olympic gold medals and three sprint world records, the suggestion was that Bolt was asking for $250,000 in appearance fees for one-off races from meeting promoters. Such demands probably limit Bolt to no more than half a dozen of the biggest track meetings that are staged each year: none of the others could afford to hire him and still manage to fill the other seven lanes in his race, Meert said.

'He is the No. 1 name,' Meert said. 'People on the street know about athletics because of him. His price is going to get higher and that is the reality we have to look at.'

Coe v Ovett, Budd v Decker, Lewis v Johnson or Lewis v Christie: the great rivalries of recent decades in athletics were rarely contested on a regular basis at the invitation meetings on the European circuit. Good intentions, and sponsors' dollars, were never enough to overcome injuries, pride and the caution of individual athletes to get them on the track at the same time, outside of championships.

Besides, since the mid-1990s, there had barely been a year go past without some form of championship event as the culmination of the athletics season. Once, there had just been the Olympics every four years, with European championships or Pan-American championships, and the Commonwealth Games staged in 'mid-term' in the Olympic cycle.

Then, in 1983, the IAAF staged its first World Championships in Helsinki, Finland. They were a phenomenal success, athletically and commercially. The Olympic Games had gone through a terrible period, scarred by terrorist attacks (in 1972 at Munich) and political boycotts (Montreal 1976 and Moscow 1980; Los Angeles in 1984 was to be similarly blighted). Thus the relatively apolitical IAAF event in 1983 was the first time a global athletics meeting had managed to go ahead with all the world's stars competing – from the United States, the Soviet Union and the eastern bloc – for more than a decade.

Helsinki was also notable for the emergence of a new global sports star: Carl Lewis. Lewis, then aged 22, won the 100 metres, long jump and 4x100 metres gold medals in the Finnish capital. He was the Usain Bolt of his day, loved by meeting promoters and sponsors alike. Only Lewis would have been able to carry off a Pirelli tyres advertisement in which the sprinter was settling into his starting blocks wearing a pair of rather fetching, scarlet stilettos. No other athlete since has enjoyed such a high profile with the broader public, until Bolt.

The success of those early World Championships prompted the then head of the IAAF, Primo Nebiolo, of Italy, to look to double his money. Short and bald, with a gravelly, heavily accented voice, unfavourable comparisons with Italian family businesses or pushy dictators were easy to make during his near-twenty-year rule over world athletics.

The IAAF World Championships were originally envisaged as being staged once every four years, occurring in the season before the Olympic Games. In 1983, 1987 and 1991, that worked well, for the sport and for the athletes. But Nebiolo wanted more: more sponsorship revenue and more TV income for the IAAF. More money for the IAAF meant more influence, and more power, for him.

'Imageen,' he would say to anyone who questioned his plan, 'we would haf twice az many world champions.'

And so, like some form of Papal edict from Rome, Nebiolo decreed that, from 1993, the IAAF would stage its track World Championships once every two years.

Twenty years on, instead of Nebiolo's plan delivering twice as many world champions, what the sport has got is many athletes, potential world stars, who have had their career spans halved, due to the unrelenting demands that the championship cycle puts on their bodies. There's little chance, though, of the IAAF cutting back on the frequency of its World Championships, since it is now entirely dependent on the income from sponsors and television.

Somewhat shrewdly, therefore, Glen Mills and 'Team Bolt' took a look at 2010 and decided it was the ideal time to give Usain Bolt an 'easier' summer, with none of the pressure – psychological as well as physical – of the training and racing in a championship year. So detached was he from the notion that he might compete at the Commonwealth Games that, by the middle of 2010, Bolt still had to be informed that the Games, in New Delhi, were to be staged in October, long after the Jamaican track season usually ends. Such a late finish to one season would, inevitably, have an impact on the start of preparation for the next year, and that was something which Mills was happy to avoid.

For the ever-relaxed Usain Bolt, 2010, therefore, would be an 'easier' year. 'I've trained hard but not with the intensity of the last two years,' he admitted in an interview early in the year.

'A break is necessary after the great events before the next ones. My trainer wanted to look at the start and other small details. This season, I'll enjoy racing against the strongest in the Golden League and it's obvious that when the best are on the track, the racing stimulus may lead to great results. But I don't have any particular aim. Or better, there is one – to enjoy myself.'

In the years since 2008, Bolt had matured as a person very quickly. He was still the party animal ('If there were gold medals for partying I'd have won every year from 2003 until I was twenty,' he once admitted), but the scale of his success and magnitude of its rewards seemed to have made him realise, quite quickly, that there is a time and a place for everything.

'Be prepared to make sacrifices,' Bolt advised in another interview given early in 2010 to help promote his ghosted biography. 'When I was starting out I had to stay at home and maintain my focus rather than going out with my friends. When you're training as hard as you can, you have to try to get your rest in the evenings.

'It was hard saying, "I'm going to stay in," while my friends were going to clubs such as Quad or Fiction in Kingston. But you have to do it. I got my own back, though – when I'm not racing I go back there, but now I know the DJs and they let me mess around on the decks at the end of the night.'

Bolt moved into a new house in Kingston in early 2010, and living there with him is Nugent Walker, or 'NJ', a lifelong friend from Trelawny and now a vital member of Team Bolt, and Sadiki, Usain's half-brother. It is as if Bolt has chosen to surround himself with good friends, to avoid the need to go out and socialise too often.

NJ, Bolt says, is now an essential link between him and the ever-growing Team Bolt: from Norman Peart, the personal manager, coach Glen Mills, agent Ricky Simms, a masseur, a finance director, even a publicist.

'You need the right people around you,' Bolt said. 'Building my success has been fairly simple, to be honest, because I have the best team. Yes, I try hard at what I do, but without them it wouldn't work.

'My family, my friends, my coach – they've all helped me to succeed. In particular, my parents were really supportive. They made sure I got to track meetings and I had everything I needed to train.

'At the same time, they made sure I trained. You knew what would happen if you didn't behave – my dad was very strict and a real disciplinarian. We feared our dad. He's big, and when we were small he instilled this fear in us.'

Bolt and his friends, who include Courtney Walsh junior, the son of the great West Indies fast bowler, and 400-metre runner Jermaine Gonzales, while away the evenings in the house, playing video games, watching sport on television – Bolt is a big fan of NBA basketball, and also famously a Manchester United supporter – and even playing dominoes, a great Caribbean passion.

For with his success and wealth, Bolt sees that he now carries considerable responsibility. 'It's important to have role models,' he said. 'When I was younger mine were Michael Johnson and Don Quarrie. Johnson was pretty much the best runner in the world, particularly at the 200 metres – my favourite event – and Quarrie was one of the best Jamaican sprinters in history, so I just wanted to be like them.'

In early 2010, the BBC sent a television crew to Jamaica with Johnson to make a film about the world's fastest man, visiting Trelawny, the Bolt family, his school and childhood haunts, and observing him training in Kingston.

In the 1990s, Johnson was the world's leading male athlete, a world record-holder at 200 and 400 metres, and the only man ever to have won the 200 and 400 metres gold medals at the same Olympic Games.

More recently, the American has developed a reputation as a trenchant observer of the sport in his expert summariser's role with BBC Sport. Over the previous couple of years, Johnson had not always been entirely complimentary about Bolt's conduct on the track. Yet he had never failed to be awed by Bolt's performances and potential.

'We had met briefly on a few occasions but this was an opportunity to really get to know each other,' Johnson said. 'I was worried he may be a little cagey about speaking, but it was surprisingly easy to get him to open up. I think a combination of things helped him relax.

'We were at his practice track, where he was in his element with familiar faces, and there was also a curiosity on his part, too. He had questions he wanted to ask me. As opposed to it being an interview, it ended up being more of a conversation.'

They say that the greatest athletes are the ones who always want to learn more. Everyone who has met Bolt observes that he has a curiosity about most things, an enquiring mind and a thirst for knowledge.

Johnson said, 'Usain told me he felt like he had not established himself, in terms of winning championships, in the way Carl Lewis or I did.'

But Johnson also formed a view that Bolt is no longer interested in trying to outdo his world records. 'He has already run so much faster than anyone in history and he doesn't need to go quicker to keep beating the other athletes,' Johnson said.

'The only way I see him losing to Tyson Gay or Asafa Powell is if Usain were to suffer from an injury, illness or if he just stops training. Usain is in control – Tyson and Asafa are not. Those guys are in a very difficult position where they don't control their own destiny. No matter what they do, they cannot beat him unless he allows it by stepping on to the track unprepared.'

Even by late 2011, it seemed much more likely that the one part of that sprint triumvirate who might be stepping on to a track underprepared would be Gay. Injuries, real or perceived, had prevented the American, the world's *second fastest* man (a title which appeared to cause Gay more discomfort than pride), from competing against Bolt on numerous occasions. It has seemed that the agonising about the injuries was as painful for Gay as the agony of the injuries themselves.

Gay will be twenty-nine years old in the Olympic year of 2012, which is hardly 'over the hill' in the modern professional sporting world. More importantly, though, it will be three years since he last toed a starting line against Bolt in decent shape at a championships. On that occasion he ran faster than he had ever raced before, and he was still left wanting.

A groin strain in Berlin had prevented Gay from defending his 200 metres world title, yet he was recovered sufficiently to race again a month later in China, when he recorded 9.69sec for another American 100 metres record. Yet still it was now only as good as Bolt's second fastest time.

Gay is coached in Florida by Lance Brauman, himself a controversial figure following a fraud conviction in 2006 which forced him to watch his athlete's double gold success at the 2007 World Championships on a television set in a jail cell.

Brauman has described competing against Bolt, for coach as well as athlete, as 'frustrating'.

'It's not like he's not running fast,' Brauman said. 'He's just trying to beat a guy that's seven inches taller than him. You do the math.'

Gay appears to have 'done the math', and when asked publicly, he seems by no means intimidated by the scale of the task before him. 'I want to own that world record one day,' he said in one interview after the Berlin championships. 'I've been so close to it. A lot of people think it is out of reach, but I'm striving to get there.

'I guess I think I can beat him,' Gay said of his nemesis. 'I've never viewed anyone as unbeatable. If anyone has beaten me, I've always worked hard to try to beat them. That's why I can beat Bolt.'

As an afterthought, Gay added, needlessly some might think: 'It isn't going to be easy though.'

Bolt used 2010 and early 2011 to make it tougher still for his opposition, doing the sort of strength and gym work which his back condition had made impossible in previous years, despite his own preferences for training sessions. 'I'll take the track over the gym any day,' Bolt said.

'A modern-day sprinter needs to be strong and fairly built up, but it's no fun having sessions in the gym. For me, time out on the track wins every time. I can't avoid going to the gym, though. It's the weights sessions I never look forward to.'

Coupling additional power to Bolt's obvious natural assets of very long levers, Michael Johnson believes, is increasing the Jamaican's potential speed.

'Having watched Usain train up close and analysed his races, I can see that he has a set of gifts that no one else has: an incredibly long stride combined with the ability to execute a race like a shorter sprinter – generating the same explosive power.

'That combination makes him so much faster than the rest of the field. But he could go faster.'

Johnson runs a speed clinic in Texas, which makes use of numerous modern video devices and computer analysis to study a sportsman's form. In Bolt's case, Johnson is convinced that his sometimes rolling gait is costing him energy, and time. 'The wasted motion causes a chain reaction that goes down through the body and creates several inefficiencies in the entire system,' Johnson said on the television programme. 'Analysing his technique in slow motion, as incredible as it may sound, shows some flaws that are glaring.'

Bolt has always maintained that he is willing, keen in fact, to learn. 'No matter how good you are, there is always room for improvement,' he said.

'Getting a good start in sprinting is very important, and it's something that's hard for me because I'm so tall. It doesn't come naturally, so I've had to practise a lot. Being tall really helps when I get going, as I've got a long stride, but it's not ideal for starting. It took me a while, but I finally got there, and now my start's a lot better.'

As the man who put the smile back on the face of international athletics, it is perhaps unsurprising that Bolt says that 'The best advice I was ever given was to always enjoy the sport. My coach told me that when I was starting out. If you enjoy what you do you can really put your heart into it.'

That, though, should stop short of the sort of behaviour Bolt routinely indulges in ahead of his races, according to none other than Carl Lewis.

Lewis, the nine-time Olympic gold medal-winner, now with ambitions in politics, told the French newspaper *L'Equipe*, 'Even for Usain Bolt, no race is won in advance. I'm not saying that to be critical, just that you have to approach every challenge with humility. When you're on top everyone wants to take your place. I won 17 gold medals in Olympics and World Championships but I missed out on some because of the strength of the competition.

'He has to concentrate on just one thing when he is out on the track: his performance. He shouldn't get distracted by all the fuss around the event or this habit athletes have now to make some sort of show for the cameras.

'When his career is over, no one will say: "I loved your attitude at the start." Rather it is: "Congratulations on all those gold medals."'

And unfortunately for Bolt, one of the gold medals which might have been his would be missing from his collection at the end of 2011 after one of the most notorious false starts in sports history.

Lewis may well have had Bolt's lower key 2010 season in mind, too, when he made his comments.

BOLT HAD OPENED the 2010 season very promisingly with a 19.56sec 200 metres performance in Kingston – the fourth-fastest run of all time. Yet an attempt at a meet staged in the Czech Republic on the 300 metres world best, set ten years earlier by Michael Johnson, not only saw Bolt walk away from the track without the record (he ran 30.97sec; he needed to go faster than 30.85) but with an Achilles tendon injury which would blight the rest of his season.

Bolt's 2010 season was curtailed before the end of July, soon after he was well beaten over 100 metres by Tyson Gay in Stockholm's historic old Olympic Stadium, the American running 9.84 to Bolt's 9.97.

After his low-key 2010, Bolt emerged for the 2011 season having bulked up noticeably across his shoulders, no longer looking like the gangly youth of 2007, 2008 or even 2009. Possibly to the dismay of Michael Johnson and his acute eye for technique, Bolt was no smoother in his running in races, though.

Bolt looked laboured on his seasonal debut in Rome on May 26. In Oslo a fortnight later, running his first 200 metres of the season, Bolt still lacked the silky fluency he had possessed when streaking to his world record in Beijing and Berlin, though he was strong enough to clock 19.86sec despite the faults.

Nonetheless, after that race he and coach Mills took the unusual step of flying back to Jamaica for a month to re-group. 'Me and my coach sat down and watched a few tapes and we worked on what we needed to work on, and I'm feeling much better,' Bolt told a press conference in Paris in July, when he returned to Europe to resume his track season. 'I'm feeling more confident.

'My technique and fluency wasn't there, my coach says, I didn't look as smooth as usual. My start was

OK but when I got into my drive phase it wasn't as fluent as it usually is.'

Bolt had been off the racetrack for a long time, too, and top racers are rarely able to perform at their best until the fourth or fifth race of their season, when they manage to rediscover their 'sharpness'. 'It's hard to come back from injury,' Bolt told the press conference. 'When I was young I got injured and people would say "he won't make it back", "he won't do well", "his career is over". But I'm now the Olympic and world champion. For me all I have to do is work hard and stay focused.

'It felt good to run 9.91 in my first race back and I ran 19.86 and I know what I need to do to get back to the top and that's what I'm working on.

'I'm working back from injury to get back to the Usain Bolt that everyone knows and loves. I want to retain my titles and become a legend in the sport. That's my aim, that's my goal this season and so I'm going to work hard and stay focused.'

One reference to himself in the third person, two mentions of how 'focused' he had become. Anyone who follows professional sport regularly will understand that these can be the worrying signs of a sports star on the wane: Bolt was either not as confident in his own ability as he was telling the world he was, or he really had been 'got at' by the marketing people. If it was the latter, then the fear must be that his earnestness and frankness from the early years of his career had been replaced by *nothingspeak*, a new language spoken fluently in corporate circles, especially cultivated to impart as little insight or information to the outside world as possible.

Bolt went on to admit that some of his problems of form over the previous eighteen months or so had been related to his back condition, scoliosis. 'I got too laid-back last season and when I get lazy and take it easy that's when I get injured.

'I backed off doing my back exercises and that's the reason I got injured last season. I have been doing a lot of work on my back and my hamstrings, on my core work. I have been putting a lot of emphasis on that this year. You should learn from your mistakes, and I have learned,' he said.

IN LESS THAN perfect conditions, Bolt duly went out and won the 200 metres at Paris's Diamond League meeting. Although he finished almost two-tenths quicker than the home favourite, Christophe Lemaitre, this was a prosaic performance by the big man, who finished outside 20 seconds. And for his build-up to Daegu and the defence of his World Championship titles, Bolt had just two more races.

During the 2011 season, whenever put up before the world's media by Grand Prix meeting promoters, Bolt was notably playing down his prospects, talking more about how injury had hampered his training. 'Given my injury and my back problems, I was a little behind,' he said ahead of his next race, a 100 metres in Monaco.

'Certainly, everyone is waiting for me. But I will apply myself to win the World Championships.

The important thing in a career is to win major championships. The clock does not matter.'

Bolt was trying hard to manage expectations.

His run in Monaco possibly showed why. Bolt was quick – 9.88sec – but only won by 0.02sec from his fellow Jamaican, Nesta Carter.

Next stop on Bolt's grand tour of Europe was back to Stockholm, scene of his defeat to Tyson Gay a year earlier. By now, it was looking as if Gay's 2011 season was already over after he pulled up injured at the US trials. So who would be Bolt's main challengers?

Over 200 metres in the Swedish capital, the immediate answer was Alonso Edwards, the young Panamanian who had finished runner-up at the previous World Championships in Berlin. Yet in Stockholm. Edward finished nearly half a second behind Bolt, as the Jamaican narrowly missed dipping under the 20sec mark.

BEFORE THEY BOARDED the plane for the long flight to Korea, there must have been more than a sense of concern even within Team Bolt about their man's recent form, as he would be going into the 100 metres in Daegu with five rivals having already run quicker in 2011, topped by Asafa Powell's 9.78sec in Lausanne at the end of June.

Even the young Yohan Blake, another member of Glen Mills' training squad, was burning up the tracks, having beaten Carter over 100 metres in London in the final European meet before Daegu, running 9.95sec into a strong headwind, measured at -1.6 metres per second.

Bolt opted for defiance in his last press conference before leaving Europe. 'I'm unbeaten this year and aim to defend all my titles in Daegu,' he said. 'I think it will be the same as Berlin. Some people ran well in the early season but it is the championships that count.'

No prizes for guessing whom he might have had in mind when he said that. 'Asafa has always been a good athlete. He has been running fast for many years and deserves a lot of respect for his achievements,' Bolt said.

The trouble was, like Gay, Powell was not getting any younger, and a groin strain had forced the twenty-eight-year-old former holder of the world record to miss the Blake race in London.

With the absence of Gay and with Bolt's form shaky at best, and with less than a month before the championships in Daegu, you sensed Powell's frustration that this, his best, perhaps last, chance of a big title, might yet be denied to him by injury. 'After a race, when you have run well,' Powell said, 'you want to put your legs away in a cupboard and just bring them out the next time you race.'

Despite the almost mechanical manner with which he has been able to rattle off sub-10sec 100-metre races – more than seventy by the end of 2011, more than anyone else in history – Powell is no Bionic Man with detachable fittings. Would his injury be serious enough to affect his running once in Korea?

Almost every press conference in the middle of the 2011 summer, regardless of who it was with or who they might be competing against, had to have at least one mandatory question about Bolt. And no one had a bad word to say about the young man who was reviving their sport.

One session with Allyson Felix, the American sprinter who had won world titles at 200 metres in 2005, 2007 and 2009, was typical. 'He has brought so much attention to track and field,' Felix said when the Bolt question was asked. 'That is a really positive thing. People who do not know anything about track and field know Bolt at least. That is fun.

'He is doing a lot of good for the sport because none of it is negative. He is doing things we have never seen; we are witnessing history.'

Yet for all the recovery work that Bolt had managed to do for the reputation of his sport, the darker history of track and field athletics somehow always seemed to be lurking in the shadows around the next corner.

So it was in late summer 2011 that, in the absence of Tyson Gay, emerging from the shadows as the main American challenger to Bolt over 100 metres would be Justin Gatlin, Bolt's predecessor as Olympic 100 metres champion, now just back after a four-year doping ban.

In his first national championships race since 2006, Gatlin had placed second to Walter Dix at the US Trials, running 9.95sec and earning himself his air ticket to Korea. His journey back had been a very long one.

In July 2006, almost two years after he had won Olympic gold in Athens, Gatlin failed a routine drugs test in Kansas. Gatlin remains convinced that he was framed, somehow set up for a fall.

Now, Gatlin wanted to show he could come back to the top level of sprinting. 'I want to go out there and do what no one's ever done – and that's recapture some kind of glory,' Gatlin said in the week before the action began in Daegu.

'I wanted to say, "You can think what you like of me because of that over there – the scandal. And now you have this victory over here – the comeback. You can judge me as you like on TV or on your blogs but just give me a lane and let me run again." I can become the best, the second best, the third best, but you know what? I've conquered this in a fashion no one's ever done before.'

Yet after three years of 'remedial work' on the sport's reputation, a successful comeback by even a pure and clean Gatlin was not very high on international athletics' wish list ahead of Daegu, and with the London Olympics less than a year away. For Bolt to be beaten at its World Championships would be shock enough, but for him to be beaten by someone who had in the past failed a drugs test would be a very tricky matter for the spin doctors at the IAAF and their sponsors.

And Gatlin's background made him the sport's least welcome guest at the Daegu feast. After all, Gatlin had been close to the heart of one of the dirtiest drug episodes in the history of athletics. Gatlin had worked closely with Trevor Graham, the Jamaican-born coach who had won a 4x400 metres relay silver medal at the 1988 Olympics and who was notoriously banned for life for his part in the BALCO scandal, when he trained Marion Jones and Tim Montgomery.

'I was a pawn in that situation,' Gatlin said. 'The link with Graham didn't help.

'I never trained with Marion Jones. Never trained with them or even stepped on the same track. I was with Shawn Crawford, Lisa Barber and Dwight Thomas. Trevor said: "Don't worry about the press. You're all legit. I've never given any of you anything. You work very hard." We believed him. At that time US Track and Field and the IAAF hadn't kicked him out. He was still a legit coach.'

When Gatlin tested positive, Graham defended the sprinter by accusing his squad's massage therapist of deliberately administering cream which contained banned steroids. As it was, following a 2001 adverse drug test, when traces of amphetamines had been found in Gatlin's urine sample – he claimed they were contained in a medication he was taking for his Attention Deficit Disorder – the sprinter might have expected a mandatory life ban for a second doping offence. The authorities instead opted to be lenient and handed down the four-year suspension, allowing him back on to the racetrack in 2011.

Gatlin had spent much of the previous three years trying to get his life back on track, in every sense. 'I was depressed about life. There were times I felt, "Who would miss me if I ran this car off the road right now?"'

But Gatlin had also watched plenty of track and field on television, from Beijing, from Berlin, and that meant he had seen lots of Bolt. The man who had once also had a share of the 100 metres world record, at 9.77sec, said: 'I was excited to watch Bolt race. I was also shocked by how fast he ran. Everyone was.'

Thursday morning in Daegu, just forty-eight hours before the starter would fire his gun for the first time at the latest edition of the IAAF World Championships. Thousands of the world's finest runners, jumpers and throwers had been arriving in the city during the previous week, a journey that for most involved a tedious wait at Seoul Airport before getting the connecting flight to take them south.

Many of the journalists sent to cover the event had travelled later, some arriving from America or Europe as late as the Wednesday night, so there was no chance to take time to recover from any jet-lag after their near-day-long journey or acclimatise to the subtropical temperatures before hurtling headlong into a round of press conferences and 'preview opportunities', arranged by national teams, the local organisers, the international federation, and some by the running shoe companies.

If you were unfortunate enough to step outside an air-conditioned hotel lobby or taxi, it was as if the 30-degree heat hit you, bouncing up from the pavement. Within minutes, in the high humidity you felt as if you were melting in your own perspiration. The next few days were going to be a hard slog.

It was hard to form an immediate impression of Daegu, beyond its seeming to be an unprepossessing sort of place. But what masked it was that it seemed to have been transformed, just for this week, into Bolt City. Every billboard, every shop front, every poster billboard had been taken up with an image of the world's fastest man.

Arriving outside the Daeduk Cultural Center there was already one TV crew and a minor traffic jam of taxis disgorging themselves of passengers. This was surely the story of the day, the preview piece for Friday, and possibly Saturday papers, too: Bolt was back.

The Jamaica team press conference, even in the years before Usain Bolt, had always been a rich source of story material ahead of championships or Olympic Games. Now, in the era of Bolt, attendance was obligatory.

And, however underwhelming some of his racing might have been in the previous weeks, Bolt's press conferences never disappoint. A day or so before, in another hired room in Daegu, Tyson Gay had made himself available. Even if you are an injured athlete, your sponsors normally want you to perform certain media functions.

The sprinter turned pundit, and in his own absence from the championships Gay had told some American reporters that he was certain that Bolt would win again in Daegu because he has a 'championship pedigree'.

When this was put to him, Bolt laughed. He always laughed, but this seemed genuinely to amuse him. 'I've proved it twice,' Bolt said, 'so I guess he knows what he's talking about.'

Bolt pulled himself up now, the grin evaporating from his face for the moment. 'At championships I believe I am much more focused. Even when I've not been doing well in training, and I've been messing up, when it comes to a championship I have a real focus because I want it really bad.'

Was Bolt actually suggesting, we wondered, that everything in his preparations had not been perfect?

'Now I want it even more because I want to be a legend,' he said. 'I've been working this week. I'm focused and I'm ready so – I'm going to get it done.' That was his second 'focus' of the press conference, and we had barely been going for three minutes. Used by sportsmen, it is an empty word, designed to tell the media nothing. Reading the subscript, clearly something was wrong.

'I'm coming back from injury and I'm working really hard to get back into tip-top shape,' he said.

So now we were learning something: if he was working hard 'to get back into tip-top shape', that suggests that he was not as race fit as he could be.

'I don't think I'm in 9.5 shape,' Bolt said, 'but I definitely will be able to run fast.' With Gay out and growing doubts about Powell's race-readiness, Bolt might run 9.7sec and still have a serious advantage come the 100 metres final on Sunday night.

'I wouldn't say it was more difficult to win than in 2009, although there's a lot of guys running fast, and I'm not in tip-top shape which I was in Berlin. But I think I'm focused and I'm ready now.'

A third 'focus' from the great man: the alarm bells are really ringing now. Maybe the rumours – someone had read something in an English-language Korean daily paper over breakfast – that he had an

Achilles tendon problem, a recurrence of the injury that ended his 2010 season, were true?

'Injury?' Bolt baulked. 'No such thing. Us athletes, we get pains every day. Your back, your leg... so then it's put some ice on it, and I'm good again. I'm great now.'

Sounds reasonable enough.

'I'm fine. For me it's just about getting back into shape. Fitness-wise I'm good. Technique – I'm almost there. I wouldn't say it was 100 per cent, but I'm happy.

'I think people expect a lot from me. To me, pressure is always there. It was there even before I won my first gold medal. But I don't look at it as pressure. I just look at it as "everyone wants the best from me" so I just go ahead and do my race.

'A lot of people have said that I am a legend, but I don't look at it like that,' he said, his unforced modesty yet again winning over his audience. Donovan Bailey, the 1996 Olympic 100 metres champion, used to have the same thing about him; easy, relaxed, refreshingly well-grounded. Bolt's the same, if not more so. What's not to like?

'But, in two years,' he adds, perhaps for the benefit of the 2012-obsessed British press in his audience, 'I'm working on it...'

He appeared genuinely flattered by the reception he had received since arriving in Daegu. 'Yeah, I've seen the pictures, they're everywhere,' he said. 'This is a first for me. There were pictures everywhere and it was like "Wow!" It kinda woke me up a little bit: this is serious. You come in here, you see a lot of people and a lot of cameras, you know that it is business.'

And it is also about history, both of the sport, and of Usain Bolt. 'Other people have won championships and other people have broken records. But only a few people have repeated that year in, year out. Especially in the sprints it's really hard to win and come back four years after that. But I've said before that that's what it's going to take to become a legend.'

And to do that, he needed to retain his title as 100 metres world champion over the coming weekend.

BUT BOLT BEING Bolt, what happened in Daegu on the evening of August 28 would ensure not just back page headlines, but would put track and field athletics on the front pages of newspapers all across the world and, in the time-honoured phrase, for all the wrong reasons.

The easiest, most obvious line would be, of course, that Usain Bolt was just too fast for his own good.

Because the 100 metres, the ultimate test of human speed, at championship level is also about cunning, composure and cleverness. Justin Gatlin, with his experience of World Championships and Olympic Games, had put it well a week or so earlier when he had said, 'I thrive in this environment where I can assess my competitors through the rounds.

'It becomes a chess match and once you reach the big show itself, the final, you can strike. What track lacks in physical contact we make up for in psychological warfare. It's all about calibrating yourself in your psyche and laying the gauntlet down to your opponents.'

In Daegu, Bolt was checkmated by his training partner, through his own super-eagerness to do well.

THE IAAF HAD changed the format of its championships for the 100 metres runners in Daegu, giving the top-ranked runners, like Bolt, a bye through what used to be called the 'first round', and a lie-in on the Saturday morning.

Instead of the first round, they now staged a preliminary round to eliminate the obvious duffers from the entries. It is a format that is also planned to be used at the London Olympic Games, denying anyone who has paid for tickets for the first session of athletics the chance of seeing Bolt, Gay and Powell in action.

Thus Bolt's entrance to his stage in Daegu was delayed until the Saturday evening, and the 100 metres quarter-finals. As he warmed up, he toyed with the crowd and the local television director. A stride down the straight was followed by a rolling stroll back, and spotting his image on the giant screen, Bolt played to the camera, stroking his early-growth of beard as if he were an aged sage.

By now, it had been confirmed that Asafa Powell had failed to recover from his injury – Bolt, despite being a part of the Jamaican team, had denied all knowledge at his previous press conference. Powell would not be starting in the 100 metres, nor would Tyson Gay. Without his two closest rivals, could matters get any easier for Bolt?

In the quarter-final, he looked like he was barely running any faster than in his warm-up strides. A more routine qualification you would probably never see: he virtually stopped racing before he had even reached halfway down the straight. Here, the Koreans were using a football stadium which had been built to stage matches in the 2002 football World Cup. The 40,000 spectators who filled all the seats on this muggy evening seemed delighted with what they saw of Bolt's demonstration 100-metre run, completed in 10.10sec, the fastest of the round. Runner-up, some way behind him, and from the exile of lane eight, was Britain's Dwain Chambers.

THE WORLD CHAMPIONSHIPS allow defending champions an automatic entry, which meant that Jamaica was able to field three other athletes in the 100 metres, and the black, green and gold colours zipped along in impressive style; the era of American dominance of the sprints appeared long gone, as Yohan Blake clocked 10.12sec, Nesta Carter 10.26, with Michael Frater, the direct beneficiary of Powell's injury absence, also a heat winner in 10.26.

In his heat, Justin Gatlin could place only second to the European champion, Christophe Lemaitre, the American being timed at 10.31. The comeback for Gatlin looked a long way off. The IAAF officials in the VIP box over the home straight seemed to stop shuffling uncomfortably in their chairs, and relaxed. Gatlin would be no threat to their favourite.

After that somewhat facile effort, the Jamaicans all got on the bus back to their hotel for some rest before the big day on Sunday.

By Sunday's evening session, it was already becoming apparent that the set-up of the stadium meant that most of the sprint sessions would be staged into a troublesome head wind. The stadium in Daegu, at the centre of a bowl of a valley, seemed to suck the air into it come the evening, so that as the sprinters took to their blocks and looked down the straight, they could feel the breeze blowing into their faces, see the flags around the stadium blowing in their direction. If the local organising committee had wanted sprint records, this was not the way to get them.

Bolt's re-emergence on the evening was marked by another thoroughbred performance, as the Jamaican seemed to grow into his joint role as superstar and cheerleader-in-chief. This time, he covered the ground as easily as you would like to see in 10.05sec, looking like a different class to his runner-up, the Frenchman, Lemaitre (10.11), as Richard Thompson – the Olympic silver medallist and one of those who had run more quickly than Bolt early season – fell by the wayside.

In the first semi-final, Blake repeated his season's best time, 9.95sec, but only after one of the outside fancies for a medal, Chambers, was disqualified for a false start. The American champion, Walter Dix, was beginning to look like a contender, as he matched Bolt's time behind Blake.

Bolt's progress towards a second 100 metres world title had appeared so comfortable that few studied the disqualification of Chambers in any great detail. Nor, perhaps, had they noticed the disqualification from a preliminary round of the women's 400 metres of Christine Ohuruogu, an Olympic and former world champion, who sulked away from the track, close to tears and in a state of shock, her year's work wrecked and ruined.

Had anyone bothered to watch more closely, had Team Bolt seen these worrying signs, they might have realised that danger lay ahead, especially for a man who had almost failed to make the 2009 World Championship final because of his own presumptive starting.

But the rules that had applied in Berlin had been changed. In fact, the false start rule, No. 162.7, had been changed twice since 2003, largely at the behest of broadcasters, whose schedules were shredded by frequent and repeated delays at race starts, where each athlete was allowed to make two false starts.

From 2003, a new rule allowed one false start among the field, but anyone false-starting thereafter would be disqualified (whether they had committed the first false start themselves or not). From 2010, the season when Usain Bolt was taking it 'easy', an even more Draconian rule was introduced, with immediate disqualification for anyone false starting.

As Simon Barnes, of the London *Times*, observed, 'Go on the "B" of the Bang. So said Linford Christie, who won the 100 metres for Great Britain at the Olympic Games of 1992. But with the Olympic Games upon us next year, it's clearly time to amend that. Go on the "A" of the Bang, or maybe the "N".

It's not such a snappy phrase but you're less likely to get disqualified.'

In the end, it seemed the only way Bolt would get beaten. When announced, Bolt played to the crowd with the camera on him, pointing to left and right and then shaking his head before pointing down his lane with both fingers and nodding. As the athletes were called to their blocks, the eight finalists, including four Jamaicans, crouched down into their positions. Bolt, as he had been all week, was at the epicentre of the action, drawn in lane five, with Dix to his left and his friend and training partner, Blake, to his right in lane six.

But before the customary hollow crack of the starter's gun could be heard echoing around the stadium, Bolt was off. He was a stride out of his blocks before any of his rivals reacted to his move. Three strides down the straight, the grimace on his face told of his realisation of what he had done. He quickly came to a near halt, almost ripping at his race vest as he sought to take it off, pull it over his face to hide his reaction from the thousands of flashbulbs that were now exploding at his discomfort.

Bolt stomped back to the start line, throwing his arms this way and that in clear frustration. Had there been any doubt in the starter's or officials' minds about a technicality, what is sometimes called a 'faulty start', Bolt had already removed it from their minds, as he had virtually put his hand up to this carnal sin of the sprinter.

In the press seats, the replays of the incident were scrutinised closely. Was there any hope for

the man whom British bookmakers had made
1-20 on favourite to win this race – meaning that
to win just a single pound or dollar, you needed
to hand Mr William Hill or Mr Ladbroke twenty
pounds or dollars in advance. It works out as five
per cent interest on your money when compared
to cash in the bank, not a bad return in less than
a day. But Bolt had just rendered his previously
confident backers' money less safe than a deposit
with Northern Rock.

The replays seemed to show that Blake, next to
Bolt, and right in his eyeline, may have twitched just
before the champion made his move. That might
have been the mitigation he needed, but if Blake's
movement was not picked up by the sensors in the
athletes' blocks...

On the track, a Korean official approached Bolt,
waving his red card. Bolt knew it was coming. Then
he was asked to leave the track, and that seemed
to be a request Bolt found hard to take. Eventually,
the soon-to-be ex-world champion exited to the
run-off area to the right of the 100 metres start,
where he proceeded to punch his fists against the
wall. Photographers, positioned at the far end of
the track for the triumphal finish of the race, had
scurried the length of the stadium to capture this
moment instead. As the official report of the event
said, 'Suddenly, the man who loved to be the centre
of attention just wanted the world to go away.'

When the starter asked the stadium for quiet for
the start, Bolt paused from his agonies and turned to
watch for ten seconds as his 100 metres world title

raced away from him. Next time people looked, Bolt had bolted.

What Bolt had seen before he disappeared into the night was Blake taking his mantle, the twenty-one-year-old seizing a world title in a moment of massive anti-climax.

Under pressure from Kim Collins in lane three, Blake had overcome his own shock at the preceding minutes' events, and over the final sixty metres produced the race of his life, clocking 9.92sec. Walter Dix, the double Olympic medallist from the United States, took silver in 10.08, with Collins, eight years after he had himself won the title, this time taking bronze, the oldest 100 metres medal-winner in the history of the World Championships.

But Tyson Gay, himself forced to watch from the sidelines, seemed to speak for many in the stadium and watching on television around the world when he said, 'Without Usain Bolt, the race is going to have an asterisk to the side.'

Chapter 7

Redemption Song

'I HAVE NOTHING to say right now. I need some time.'

Usain Bolt had headed out to the warm-up track to collect his belongings, to collect his thoughts.

For a sportsman usually so obliging to the media, Bolt had made sure that he bypassed the Mixed Zone, and, as soon as he was ready, he made use of an official car to get back to the privacy of his accommodation. With the help of Ricky Simms and the Puma press operation, the IAAF issued a statement on Bolt's behalf a couple of hours later. As 'no comments' go, it pretty well covered the bases. How would he be in the 200 metres? 'We'll find out on Friday,' he said.

Bolt was a swirl of conflicting emotions, because as well as his own frustration and anger at himself, he also probably did not want to do anything that might detract from the moment for his friend, Yohan Blake. Yet he could not help continuing to be the centre of attention. Bolt was the story, whether he liked it or not.

So when Blake arrived for his champion's press conference, his questions were all about the champion-who-was-no-more. 'When he did the false start I was so surprised because we had been talking about that in training,' Blake said.

'He false-starts a lot – and now it happens. I knew I would challenge Bolt one day but I did not expect it today. I am traumatised and I have mixed feelings.'

Michael Johnson, in Daegu working for British broadcaster Channel 4, having been won over by Bolt during his earlier visit to Jamaica, now turned critic again. 'I don't think it's too much to ask to wait until the gun goes before you go off,' Johnson said.

'I wonder if he had kept his shirt on and kept his calm and walked back to the blocks, if they wouldn't have tried to find some kind of excuse to keep him in the contest?' Johnson asked.

The cynics like Johnson were matched in equal number by the depressives, those saddened by the stern and unyielding fate suffered by Bolt. 'Now, because of an ill-devised rule, because of a depressing and rather inhuman policy of zero tolerance, athletics has spoiled the greatest thing it possesses,' *The Times* suggested. 'Sport brings heartbreak: it's supposed to and it does it often. It's right that losing should break hearts: but the same penalty surely should not apply to twitching.'

To all those who were questioning its wisdom, the IAAF worked late into the night to produce its own justification for the false-start rule.

'While the IAAF is, of course, disappointed that Usain Bolt false-started in the final of the 100 metres,' Nick Davies, the federation's spokesman, said formally, 'it is important to remember that a sport's credibility depends on its rules, and they must also be applied consistently and fairly for *all* athletes.'

Informally, speaking with a gaggle of reporters by the press conference room, Davies made an important point. 'It's sport, not showbusiness. You have to be careful about saying, "This is our big star and he needs protecting for the sake of entertainment."

'Respect for the rules has to be paramount.'

Yes, said Davies, the IAAF's governing council would discuss the situation. But would they, could they, be seen to change the rule now, in direct response to Bolt's disqualification, when they had worked hard to get the support for the change from so many coaches and athletes – including from Bolt himself?

In any case, this had been no marginal jumping of the gun. Bolt had blasted a full one-tenth of a second before the starter had pulled his trigger. The start is always a key factor in any sprint race, but for Bolt, we know, his physical dimensions have always made it extra critical, to enable him to unravel his 6ft 5in frame and unleash his ground-eating stride as soon as possible.

Yet Bolt had a record of not just getting *good* starts, but of getting *very good* starts, getting the jump on his rivals, as he had done against Tyson Gay in the previous World Championship 100 metres final in Berlin two years earlier. If, as Blake suggested, Bolt false-started a lot in training sessions, were his race-day performances the result of super-quick reflexes, or in fact just the by-product of repeated practice to anticipate the starter's signal?

Certainly, there are many sprinters who, as a matter of routine, sit in the stands at a track meeting and listen to the rhythm and cadence of the starter as he calls his instructions. 'Take your marks... Set...' Does he wait two beats, or is it three, before he pulls the trigger?

Even in rugby union, front row forwards try to learn the beat of instructions from their referees before a scrum, who bark 'Crouch, touch, pause... Engage!', so that they might better time their headlong thrust into the opposition pack's shoulders and thus get them on to the back foot.

Might, on this occasion, have Bolt been taking a chance, to ensure a quick break and to impose himself on Blake and Dix as soon as possible in the race? For a man whose own form coming to the Daegu championships had not been electric, was Bolt seeking an extra spark too much?

As it was, the $60,000 first prize fund at least stayed within the same training group, and would surely have been much appreciated by Blake, who had suffered a rough 2009 following his positive test for a stimulant.

His win in Daegu, at 21 years and 244 days, made Blake the youngest 100 metres world champion in history. 'I've been waiting for this my whole life,' Blake said.

'My goal this year was to work my way up to the top. With the Olympics coming up, I'm thinking about that from now.'

Of course, after the dramatic manner in which Blake had taken the world title, a championship re-match against the reigning Olympic 100 metres champion suddenly becomes a much more intriguing possibility.

The following morning, in the light of day (they don't do 'cold light' in Daegu, even at dawn), someone at Team Bolt must have re-read the statement rushed out the previous evening and decided that 'terse' is not a word that they want associated with the world's fastest man.

So another statement was emailed to the press pack and copied and distributed among the media seats in the stadium. It quickly attended to the one element that had been so blatantly overlooked the night before: 'Firstly I would like to congratulate my team mate Yohan Blake and the other athletes who won the medals,' Bolt was reported to have said.

'Of course I am extremely disappointed not to have had the chance to defend my title due to the false start. I was feeling great through the rounds and was ready to run fast in the final. I worked very hard to get ready for this championships and things were looking good.

'However I have to move on now as there is no point to dwell on the past. I have a few days to refocus and get ready for the 200 metres on Friday. After this I have the 4x100 metres and a few other races before the end of the season. I know that I am now in good shape and will focus on running well in the 200 metres.

'Thanks to all the people who sent me good wishes and I will try my best to make you proud in the 200 metres.'

Less formally, when upbraided by a television crew on his way from the track after another routine qualifying performance in the semi-finals of the 200 metres, Bolt provided more context when asked if he had got over his 100 metres disappointment. 'Does it look like it?' Bolt said, almost as a challenge.

But then he opted to expand. 'Listen... For me, it's all business, it's a job,' Bolt said. 'You win some, you lose some. I'm over that now. You gotta move fast. You're not going to win everything. I made a mistake. I've gotta move on past that.'

The Daegu heat and humidity, rather more than the effort of his race a few minutes before, saw perspiration dripping down Bolt's face, and he wiped it away with the inside of his yellow Jamaica vest. 'I might find that I'm always feeling tired for some reason,' he said. 'But as soon as I go home and get a good night's rest, tomorrow I should feel great.'

The 'tomorrow', Saturday, September 3, would bring the final of the 200 metres, and a chance for redemption for Bolt.

It came for him in just 19.40 seconds.

It was good enough to make Michael Johnson voice considerable respect. 'He makes the performance of a lifetime an annual event,' the American said.

It may not have been Bolt's fastest ever run at his favourite distance. It 'only' got to fourth on the all-time list. But as a means of purging his psyche of any demons that had existed from earlier in the week, this was as good a way to do it as any.

Bolt had laid his starting demons. 'The start wasn't a pressure because all I had to do was sit in and wait,' he said. Patience and a touch of wisdom: he had lingered in his blocks, with the slowest reaction time of the eight finalists.

He had also watched the evening's earlier races carefully, too, and noticed that, at last, he would not have to encounter a headwind. 'I was like, "That's a good sign." I decided why not come out here and run as hard as possible?

'Lane three was a bit tight for me. I didn't run the perfect corner, I think that was the problem. If I run a good corner, I could have done much better, but I'm happy.'

And then we were re-introduced to the Bolt of old, perhaps a touch brash, but certainly, fairly, confident in his own abilities. 'I've proved to the world I am still the best. I made a mistake in the 100 metres. If I didn't I would have won, without a doubt.'

What was most impressive, perhaps, about Bolt's 200 metres victory was that he had managed to re-compose himself after the disappointments of Sunday night.

In terms of turning things around, for probably the best comparison within athletics in the modern era, you need to go back more than thirty years, to the Moscow Olympics in 1980. There, early in the week's track action, they staged the men's 800 metres. The red-hot favourite to win was the world record-holder, Sebastian Coe. Yet he ran the race of a novice – his own father basically called him an idiot – and lost to his British rival, Steve Ovett.

The defeat for Coe was both shocking and traumatic. But he had another race to come at the end of the Games, the 1500 metres, for which Ovett was the more fancied. As we all well know, Coe duly overcame his disappointment, pulled himself together, learned his lesson and won the gold medal. The comeback from adversity is always such a strong story to write.

In the case of Bolt and the Daegu 200 metres final, he delivered a rock-solid, safe start, and ran what he called a 'conservative' bend. Bolt's long legs are not used to being asked to race anywhere other than in lanes four, five or six, but because he had not bust a gut to win his semi-final, he did not get that privilege. Not that it really mattered.

As he entered the straight, the American, Walter Dix, one lane to his outside, looked poised to issue a challenge. But it was then that Bolt flew away, as if hurled down the home straight by centrifugal force.

Bolt dragged Dix through to 19.70, his fastest time since 2007 and his second silver medal of the week, and chasing hard saw Christophe Lemaitre set a French record 19.80 for third.

For a man who can run close to 25mph, what followed was possibly one of the slowest laps of honour yet witnessed. It took forty minutes after he finished the race, made a few diversions to shake hands with people in the crowd and jigged and danced his way through trackside interviews before leaving the scene.

At one point during his lap of honour, Bolt hopped over the track hoardings. He was instantly engulfed by a swarm of cameramen. When Bolt went right, they followed; so he went left, and they followed again; so now he moved to his right, as if he was playing a kitten with a ball of yarn.

He was still enjoying the appreciative screams of thousands of South Korean fans. 'The local girls were screaming like they were in the front row of the Shea Stadium in 1965,' the *Guardian* newspaper observed.

Likewise, Bolt's post-race press conference was pandemonium. It was already getting on for 11 p.m., and the following day, the final day of the Daegu championships, a fresh, fit and limber Bolt would be expected to team up with Blake and his Jamaican relay squad and race once again.

But this would be probably the first and only chance for most of the world's press to get to hear what Bolt might have to say about the preceding week's events. There must have been at least five hundred hacks crushed into the conference room. Back page and front page, Bolt was still headline news.

As is the case with such formalised press conferences, here with translations of questions and answers also being offered in Korean for the home country's reporters, the opening consisted of some politely routine enquiries, focused on his most recent race. 'I always do my best and run as hard as possible, so I'm happy,' Bolt said.

'It was a little bit different running in lane three, I don't think I have ever run in lane three before, normally it's five or six, there's a tighter turn. I was slowest out so that is not good, I was a bit tight and more conscious it was not a perfect start.'

Ah, the start. Once Bolt had mentioned the start himself, the question of his 100 metres was on the agenda. 'I have worked hard on my start all season. In the first round of the 100 metres it was perfect, in the second it was OK.

'In the final it was anxiety. I felt so good. I was ready to go. I was excited. I just wanted to get on the track and run. So personally I think anxiety got the best of me.

'I was in the blocks and when he said "set," a second after that I swear I heard someone say "Go!" So for me, it was all my fault.

'People are saying that Yohan twitched, but that is not the case. Blake has worked hard all season and if anybody deserves to win it was Yohan. Right from the moment he came to work with us he has worked hard.'

Bolt would not even make a call for the false start rule to be changed. 'I'm not going to say it should be changed. But for me I will remember this. It has taught me a lesson just to relax and stay in the blocks. My coach has been telling me this for months, to wait and listen, not try to anticipate.

'I've learned.' Redemption, writ large.

Would he tone done the pre-race antics, perhaps? 'I never stress about clowning around. It is just random stuff. It's my personality coming out. It is not planned. If it were, it would not be fun.'

So that'll be a 'No' then.

But he did concede that the Daegu championships had been less than ideal conditions for him and the rest of the sprinters. 'It has been difficult here. The majority of the time there has been a negative wind and I have not been in the best of shape, so I think it is a wonderful achievement to run 19.40.'

And what sort of time might he have managed over 100 metres? 'The way I was feeling, I would have run 9.7 or 9.6.'

There was not a flicker of surprise when Bolt said that from Dix or Lemaitre, the two other medallists forced, by protocol, to sit through all this when everyone knew that they were never going to be the story, not even for the man from the *New York Times* or the chap from *L'Equipe*. In the half-hour that we had been there, the Frenchman and American had had three questions put to them. So when Bolt assessed what he might have been able to run in the 100 metres, Dix and Lemaitre's lack of reaction was either because they had stopped listening twenty minutes earlier, or because they knew what he said was true.

And with that, Bolt was off. There would be a late start for Bolt and his relay teammates on Sunday, but it was already edging toward midnight when he was taken off in an official car, back to the athletes' village and a late supper of chicken nuggets, as once again Bolt had found an Asian cuisine which did not agree with his stomach.

The fast-food diet showed no signs of slowing him down, though. Daegu had to wait until the very final event of the nine-day programme for its first world record. But with his final race of the championships, Usain Bolt delivered.

Races run in lanes are not supposed to be a contact sport, but in the 4x100 metres relay final two of Jamaca's closest challengers, the Americans and the British, were left sprawling over the track when Darvis Patton, running the third leg, crashed into the solid figure of Harry Aikines-Aryeetey, en route to passing the baton to Dix. Patton crashed to the floor at high speed, impeding the Trinidad and Tobago team as well.

With Bolt flying down the home straight on the anchor leg, the elimination of three other contenders only served to exaggerate further the appearance of Jamaica's margin of victory: after they stopped the clock at 37.04 – 0.06sec inside the time the Jamaican quartet had run in Beijing in 2008 – it was more than one second before the runners-up, France, finished.

Only Asafa Powell was missing from the Beijing quartet, having been replaced by Yohan Blake. Nesta Carter and Michael Frater fed Yohan had set up Bolt and yet again he delivered. Front pages, back pages, Bolt is always the story.

The imperfections of Daegu for Bolt seemed to have tweaked his attention enough to make London, and the 2012 Olympic Games, even more important to him than they already were, if that is possible.

'I will be more determined next year because I missed out in the 100 metres,' Bolt said soon after Daegu. 'I have to really make an impact in London to be a legend in the sport.'

Legend: would Bolt really supplant Marley as the greatest Jamaican of all time were he to win another three Olympic golds?

'For me the Olympics is going to be a big milestone. There is not going to be any joking around in the season. I'm going to be serious. I'm going to be ready.

'I've just got to go to the Olympics now and do my best and try to blow people's minds.'

Back page or front page, come the 2012 Olympics, expect Usain Bolt to be the story.

Usain Bolt

b 21 Aug 1986
1.96m tall
88kg

100m

time	wind speed	place	venue	Date
2007				
10.03	0.7	1r1	Réthimno	18 Jul
2008				
10.03	1.8	1r1	Spanish Town	8 Mar
9.76	1.8	1r2	Kingston	3 May
9.92	0.6	1r2	Port-of-Spain	17 May
9.72 WR	1.7	1rA	New York	31 May
10.19	1.0	1h1	Kingston	27 Jun
10.40	-2.0	1s2	Kingston	28 Jun
9.85	-0.1	1	Kingston	28 Jun
9.89	0.4	2rA	Stockholm	22 Jul
10.20	-0.2	1h1	Beijing	15 Aug
9.92	0.1	1q4	Beijing	15 Aug
9.69 WR	0.0	1	Beijing	16 Aug
9.85	-0.1	1s1	Beijing	16 Aug
9.83	-0.5	1rA	Zürich	29 Aug
9.77	-1.3	1	Brussels	5 Sep
2009				
9.93	2.3	1r1	Spanish Town	14 Mar
9.91+	0.1	1rA	Manchester	17 May
10.00	-0.9	1	Toronto	11 Jun
9.77	2.1	1rA	Ostrava	17 Jun
10.14	-1.6	1h1	Kingston	26 Jun
10.11	-0.6	1s1	Kingston	27 Jun
9.86	-0.2	1	Kingston	27 Jun
9.79	-0.2	1	Saint-Denis	17 Jul
10.31	-2.9	2h2	London	24 Jul
9.91	-1.7	1	London	24 Jul
10.20	-0.5	1h9	Berlin	15 Aug
10.03	0.1	2q5	Berlin	15 Aug
9.58WR	0.9	1	Berlin	16 Aug
9.89	0.2	1s1	Berlin	16 Aug
9.81	0.0	1rA	Zürich	28 Aug

Statistics

2010

9.86	0.1	1	Daegu	19 May
9.82	0.5	1	Lausanne	8 Jul
9.84	-0.3	1	Saint-Denis	16 Jul
10.10	-0.7	1h1	Stockholm	6 Aug
9.97	0.0	2	Stockholm	6 Aug

2011

9.91	0.6	1	Rome	26 May
9.91	-0.2	1	Ostrava	31 May
9.88	1.0	1	Monaco	22 Jul
10.10	-0.7	1h6	Daegu	27 Aug
DQ	-1.4		Daegu	28 Aug
10.05	-1.0	1s2	Daegu	28 Aug
9.85	0.1	1	Zagreb	13 Sep
9.76	1.3	1	Brussels	16 Sep

150m straight

2009

14.35WB	1.1	1rA	Manchester	17 May

200m

2001

22.04	1.0	2-17	Kingston	7 Apr
21.96	-1.4	2h1-17	Bridgetown	16 Apr
21.81	-1.7	2-17	Bridgetown	16 Apr

2002

21.25		0.1	1h1-17	Nassau	31 Mar
21.12		-0.5	1-17	Nassau	1 Apr
21.61		-2.0	1-17	Kingston	20 Apr
21.13		-0.7	1-19	Kingston	22 Jun
21.34		0.3	1h2-17	Bridgetown	6 Jul
20.61		-0.4	1-17	Bridgetown	7 Jul
20.58	WYB15	1.4	1h4-19	Kingston	18 Jul
20.85		-2.5	1s2-19	Kingston	19 Jul
20.61		0.9	1-19	Kingston	19 Jul

2003

20.3h		1	Montego Bay	18 Feb
21.33	2.2	1-19	Spanish Town	1 Mar
21.42	4.2	1h1-19	Spanish Town	1 Mar
20.81	1.3	1h6-18	Kingston	2 Apr

20.25	1.9	1-18	Kingston	5 Apr
21.28	0.0	1s2-18	Kingston	5 Apr
21.02	5.0	1h2--19	Port-of-Spain	20 Apr
20.43	-1.1	1-19	Port-of-Spain	21 Apr
21.1h		1	Spanish Town	14 Jun
20.80	-1.8	1h2	Kingston	21 Jun
20.28	0.2	1	Kingston	21 Jun
21.12	-0.4	1h1-17	Sherbrooke	12 Jul
20.40	-1.1	1-17	Sherbrooke	13 Jul
21.08	-3.2	1s3-17	Sherbrooke	13 Jul
20.13 WJR WYR	0.0	1-19	Bridgetown	20 Jul
20.67	0.0	1h1-19	Bridgetown	20 Jul

2004

20.78	1.7	1-19	Spanish Town	13 Mar
21.28	0.1	1h4-19	Spanish Town	13 Mar
19.93 WJR	1.4	1-19	Hamilton	11 Apr
21.05	0.0	5h4	Athens	24 Aug

2005

20.51	1.4	1r1	Tallahassee FL	9 Apr
20.14	0.9	1	Kingston	7 May
20.31	-0.6	1	New York	11 Jun
20.90	-0.7	1h1	Kingston	24 Jun
20.91	-1.6	1s1	Kingston	26 Jun
20.27	0.5	1	Kingston	26 Jun
20.69	0.3	2s1	Nassau	10 Jul
21.00	-0.4	1h4	Nassau	10 Jul
20.03	1.8	1	Nassau	11 Jul
19.99	1.8	2	London	22 Jul
20.80	-0.4	1h5	Helsinki	9 Aug
20.87	-3.7	2q3	Helsinki	10 Aug
20.68	-0.1	4s1	Helsinki	10 Aug
26.27	-0.5	8	Helsinki	11 Aug

2006

20.08	1.5	1	Fort-de-France	29 Apr
20.10	1.3	1	Kingston	6 May
20.28	0.5	1	Ostrava	30 May
20.25	0.4	2	New York	3 Jun
20.69	1.9	1r1	New York	11 Jun
19.88	0.4	3	Lausanne	11 Jul
20.29	2.5	2r1	Réthimno	21 Jul
20.54	0.2	4	London	28 Jul
20.51	-0.5	2-22	Zürich	18 Aug

20.49		-0.2	1	Zagreb	31 Aug
20.10		-0.1	3	Stuttgart	10 Sep
19.96		0.1	2	Athína	17 Sep

2007

19.96		1.0	1r2	Port-of-Spain	27 May
19.89		1.3	2	New York	2 Jun
19.75	AR	0.2	1	Kingston	24 Jun
20.50		-2.7	1h1	Kingston	24 Jun
20.11		0.0	2	Lausanne	10 Jul
20.08		1.2	2	Sheffield	15 Jul
20.06		-0.1	1	London	3 Aug
20.12		0.0	2h4	Osaka	28 Aug
20.13		-0.3	1q2	Osaka	28 Aug
20.03		-0.4	1s1	Osaka	29 Aug
19.91		-0.8	2	Osaka	30 Aug
20.19		0.2	2	Zürich	7 Sep
20.14		0.7	3	Bruxelles	14 Sep

2008

19.83		0.3	1	Ostrava	12 Jun
20.66		-1.6	1h1	Kingston	29 Jun
19.97		1.7	1	Kingston	29 Jun
19.67	AR	-0.5	1	Athína	13 Jul
19.76		-0.4	1	London	26 Jul
20.64		-0.1	2h5	Beijing	18 Aug
20.29		0.1	1q1	Beijing	18 Aug
20.09		0.1	1s2	Beijing	19 Aug
19.30	WR	-0.9	1	Beijing	20 Aug
19.63		-0.9	1	Lausanne	2 Sep

2009

20.75		-3.6	1h1	Kingston	28 Jun
20.25		-2.4	1	Kingston	28 Jun
19.59		-0.9	1rA	Lausanne	7 Jul
20.70		-0.2	1h5	Berlin	18 Aug
20.41		0.0	1q1	Berlin	18 Aug
20.08		0.0	1s1	Berlin	19 Aug
19.19	WR	-0.3	1	Berlin	20 Aug
19.57		0.0	1	Bruxelles	4 Sep
19.68		-0.3	1	Thessaloníki	13 Sep

2010

19.56		-0.8	1	Kingston	1 May
19.76		-0.8	1	Shanghai	23 May

Usain Bolt

2011

19.86	0.7	1	Oslo	9 Jun
20.03	-0.6	1	Saint-Denis	8 Jul
20.03	-1.2	1	Stockholm	29 Jul
20.30	-0.3	1h2	Daegu	2 Sep
20.31	-1.0	1s2	Daegu	2 Sep
19.40	0.8	1	Daegu	3 Sep

300m

2010

30.97 AR		1	Ostrava	27 May

400m

2001

48.28	2-17	Bridgetown	14 Apr

2002

47.33	1-17	Nassau	30 Mar
47.4h	1-17	Kingston	20 Apr
47.12	1-17	Bridgetown	5 Jul
48.00	1h2-17	Bridgetown	5 Jul

2003

47.82	2-19	Spanish Town	1 Mar
47.94	2s1-18	Kingston	4 Apr
45.35	1-18	Kingston	5 Apr
46.35	1-19	Port-of-Spain	19 Apr
48.64	2h1-19	Port-of-Spain	19 Apr
48.36	2h2-17	Sherbrooke	10 Jul
DNS	s1-17	Sherbrooke	11 Jul

2006

48.5h	1	Kirkvine	14 Jan
47.58	3	Kingston	28 Jan

2007

45.92	1r1	Kingston	10 Feb
45.62	1rB	Baie Mahault	1 May
45.28	3r2	Kingston	5 May

2008

46.94	1r10	Kingston	26 Jan

2009

46.35	1	Kingston	14 Feb
45.54	1r4	Kingston	21 Feb

2010

45.87	1r4	Kingston	13 Feb

WORLD RECORD PROGRESSION AT 100 METRES AND 200 METRES

From 1977, all records at sprint distances up to 400 metres have been accepted only if timed fully automatically. Prior to that date the best hand-timed results have been listed.

100 Metres

Record	Name and Nationality	Venue	Date
10.6	Donald Lippincott (USA)	Stockholm	6 Jul 1912
10.6	Jackson Scholz (USA)	Stockholm	16 Sep 1920
10.4	Charles Paddock (USA)	Redlands	23 Apr 1921
10.4	Eddie Tolan (USA)	Stockholm	8 Aug 1929
10.4	Eddie Tolan (USA)	København	25 Aug 1929
10.3	Percy Williams (CAN)	Toronto	9 Aug 1930
10.3	Eddie Tolan (USA)	Los Angeles	1 Aug 1932
10.3	Ralph Metcalfe (USA)	Budapest	12 Aug 1933
10.3	Eulace Peacock (USA)	Oslo	6 Aug 1934
10.3	Christiaan Berger (NED)	Amsterdam	26 Aug 1934
10.3	Ralph Metcalfe (USA)	Osaka	15 Sep 1934
10.3	Ralph Metcalfe (USA)	Dairen	23 Sep 1934
10.3	Takayoshi Yoshioka (JPN)	Tokyo	15 Jun 1935
10.2	Jesse Owens (USA)	Chicago	20 Jun 1936
10.2	Harold Davis (USA)	Compton	6 Jun 1941
10.2	Lloyd LaBeach (PAN)	Fresno	15 May 1948
10.2	'Barney' Ewell (USA)	Evanston	9 Jul 1948
10.2	McDonald Bailey (GBR)	Belgrade	25 Aug 1951
10.2	Heinz Fütterer (FRG)	Yokohama	31 Oct 1954
10.2	Bobby Morrow (USA)	Houston	19 May 1956
10.2	Ira Murchison (USA)	Compton	1 Jun 1956
10.2	Bobby Morrow (USA)	Bakersfield	22 Jun 1956
10.2	Ira Murchison (USA)	Los Angeles	29 Jun 1956
10.2	Bobby Morrow (USA)	Los Angeles	29 Jun 1956
10.1	Willie Williams (USA)	Berlin	3 Aug 1956
10.1	Ira Murchison (USA)	Berlin	4 Aug 1956
10.1	Leamon King (USA)	Ontario, CA	20 Oct 1956
10.1	Leamon King (USA)	Santa Ana	27 Oct 1956

Usain Bolt

10.1	Ray Norton (USA)	San Jose	18 Apr 1959
10.0	Armin Hary (FRG)	Zürich	21 Jun 1960
10.0	Harry Jerome (CAN)	Saskatoon	15 Jul 1960
10.0	Horacio Esteves (VEN)	Caracas	15 Aug 1964
10.0	Bob Hayes (USA)	Tokyo	15 Oct 1964
10.0	Jim Hines (USA)	Modesto	27 May 1967
10.0	Enrique Figuerola (CUB)	Budapest	17 Jun 1967
10.0	Paul Nash (RSA)	Krugersdorp	2 Apr 1968
10.0	Oliver Ford (USA)	Albuquerque	31 May 1968
10.0	Charlie Greene (USA)	Sacramento	20 Jun 1968
10.0	Roger Bambuck (FRA)	Sacramento	20 Jun 1968
9.9	Jim Hines (USA)	Sacramento	20 Jun 1968
9.9	Ronnie Ray Smith (USA)	Sacramento	20 Jun 1968
9.9	Charlie Greene (USA)	Sacramento	20 Jun 1968
9.9	Jim Hines (USA)	Mexico City	14 Oct 1968
9.9	Eddie Hart (USA)	Eugene	1 Jul 1972
9.9	Rey Robinson (USA)	Eugene	1 Jul 1972
9.9	Steve Williams (USA)	Los Angeles	21 Jun 1974
9.9	Silvio Leonard (CUB)	Ostrava	5 Jun 1975
9.9	Steve Williams (USA)	Siena	16 Jul 1975
9.9	Steve Williams (USA)	Berlin	22 Aug 1975
9.9	Steve Williams (USA)	Gainesville	27 Mar 1976
9.9	Harvey Glance (USA)	Columbia	3 Apr 1976
9.9	Harvey Glance (USA)	Baton Rouge	1 May 1976
9.9	Don Quarrie (JAM)	Modesto	22 May 1976

Automatic timing:

9.95	Jim Hines (USA)	Mexico City	14 Oct 1968
9.93	Calvin Smith (USA)	Colorado Springs	3 Jul 1983
9.92	Carl Lewis (USA)	Seoul	24 Sep 1988
9.90	Leroy Burrell (USA)	New York	14 Jun 1991
9.86	Carl Lewis (USA)	Tokyo	25 Aug 1991
9.85	Leroy Burrell (USA)	Lausanne	6 Jul 1994
9.84	Donovan Bailey (CAN)	Atlanta	27 Jul 1996
9.79	Maurice Greene (USA)	Athens	16 Jun 1999
9.77	Asafa Powell (JAM)	Athens	14 Jun 2005
9.77	Asafa Powell (JAM)	Gateshead	11 Jun 2006
9.77	Asafa Powell (JAM)	Zürich	18 Aug 2006
9.74	Asafa Powell (JAM)	Rieti	9 Sep 2007
9.72	Usain Bolt (JAM)	New York	31 May 2008
9.69	Usain Bolt (JAM)	Beijing	16 Aug 2008
9.58	Usain Bolt (JAM)	Berlin	16 Aug 2009

Annulled by IAAF:

9.83	Ben Johnson (CAN)	Rome	30 Aug 1987

200 Metres

y denotes 220 yards time equal to or better than the existing metric record

Statistics

21.2y	William Applegarth (GBR)	London	14 Jul 1914
20.6y	Andy Stanfield (USA)	Philadelphia	26 May 1951
20.6	Andy Stanfield (USA)	Los Angeles	28 Jun 1952
20.6	Thane Baker (USA)	Bakersfield	23 Jun 1956
20.6	Bobby Morrow (USA)	Melbourne	27 Nov 1956
20.6	Manfred GerMar (FRG)	Wuppertal	1 Oct 1958
20.6y	Ray Norton (USA)	Berkeley	19 Mar 1960
20.6	Ray Norton (USA)	Philadelphia	30 Apr 1960
20.5y	Peter Radford GBR	Wolverhampton	28 May 1960
20.5	Stone Johnson (USA)	Palo Alto	2 Jul 1960
20.5	Ray Norton (USA)	Palo Alto	2 Jul 1960
20.5	Livio Berruti (ITA)	Rome	3 Sep 1960
20.5	Livio Berruti (ITA)	Rome	3 Sep 1960
20.5y	Paul Drayton (USA)	Walnut	23 Jun 1962
20.3y	Henry Carr (USA)	Tempe	23 Mar 1963
20.2y	Henry Carr (USA)	Tempe	4 Apr 1964
20.0y	Tommie Smith (USA)	Sacramento	11 Jun 1966
19.8	Tommie Smith (USA)	Mexico City	16 Oct 1968
19.8	Don Quarrie (JAM)	Calí	3 Aug 1971
19.8	Don Quarrie (JAM)	Eugene	7 Jun 1975

Automatic timing:

19.83	Tommie Smith (USA)	Mexico City	16 Oct 1968
19.72	Pietro Mennea (ITA)	Mexico City	12 Sep 1979
19.66	Michael Johnson (USA)	Atlanta	23 Jun 1996
19.32	Michael Johnson (USA)	Atlanta	1 Aug 1996
19.30	Usain Bolt (JAM)	Beijing	20 Aug 2008
19.19	Usain Bolt (JAM)	Berlin	20 Aug 2009

Note that it was not until 1951 that the IAAF first distinguished between records made on a full turn and those marks made on a straight track, which would be c.0.3-0.4 faster. Records were accepted by the IAAF for 200m and 220y on straight tracks until 1975 – the final record (at 220 yards) was 19.5 by Tommie Smith at San Jose on 7 May 1966.

4x100m

42.3	Germany	Stockholm	8 Jul 1912
42.2	USA	Antwerp	22 Aug 1920
42.0	Great Britain	Paris	12 Jul 1924
42.0	Netherland	Paris	12 Jul 1924
41.0	USA	Paris	13 Jul 1924
41.0y	Newark AC	Lincoln, Nebraska	4 Jul 1927
41.0	Eintracht Frankfurt	Halle	10 Jun 1928
41.0	USA	Amsterdam	5 Aug 1928
41.0	Germany	Berlin	2 Sep 1928
40.8	SC Charlottenburg	Breslau	22 Jul 1929
40.8y	USC	Fresno	9 May 1931

40.6	Germany	Kassel	14 Jun 1932
40.0	USA	Los Angeles	7 Aug 1932
39.8	USA	Berlin	9 Aug 1936
39.5	USA	Melbourne	01 Dec 1956
39.5	FRG	Cologne	29 Aug 1958
39.5	FRG	Rome	7 Sep 1960
39.5	FRG	Rome	8 Sep 1960
39.1	USA	Moscow	15 Jul 1961
39.0	USA	Tokyo	21 Oct 1964
38.6y	USC	Provo	17 Jun 1967
38.6	Jamaica	Mexico City	19 Oct 1968
38.3	Jamaica	Mexico City	19 Oct 1968
38.2	USA	Mexico City	20 Oct 1968
38.19	USA	Munich	10 Sep 1972
38.03	USA	Düsseldorf	13 Sep 1977
37.86	USA	Helsinki	10 Aug 1983
37.83	USA	Los Angeles	11 Aug 1984
37.79	France	Split	1 Sep 1990
37.79	Santa Monica TC	Monte Carlo	3 Aug 1991
37.67	USA	Zürich	7 Aug 1991
37.50	USA	Tokyo	1 Sep 1991
37.40	USA	Barcelona	8 Aug 1992
37.40	USA	Stuttgart	21 Aug 1993
37.10	Jamaica	Beijing	22 Aug 2008
37.04	Jamaica	Daegu	4 Sep 2011

OLYMPIC CHAMPIONS AT 100 METRES AND 200 METRES & 4x100 METRES RELAY

100 Metres

1896	Thomas Burke (USA)	12.0
1900	Frank Jarvis (USA)	11.0
1904	Archie Hahn (USA)	11.0
1906	Archie Hahn (USA)	11.2
1908	Reginald Walker (RSA)	10.8
1912	Ralph Craig (USA)	10.8
1920	Charles Paddock (USA)	10.8
1924	Harold Abrahams (GBR)	10.6
1928	Percy Williams (CAN)	10.8
1932	Eddie Tolan (USA)	10.3 (10.38)
1936	Jesse Owens (USA)	10.3
1948	Harrison Dillard (USA)	10.3
1952	Lindy Remigino (USA)	10.4
1956	Bobby Joe Morrow (USA)	10.5
1960	Armin Hary (GER)	10.2 (10.32)

Statistics

1964	Bob Hayes (USA)	10.0 (10.06)[1]
1968	James Hines (USA)	9.9 (9.95)
1972	Valeri Borzov (URS)	10.14
1976	Hasely Crawford (TRI)	10.06
1980	Allan Wells (GBR)	10.25
1984	Carl Lewis (USA)	9.99
1988	Carl Lewis (USA)	9.92[2]
1992	Linford Christie (GBR)	9.96
1996	Donovan Bailey (CAN)	9.84
2000	Maurice Greene (USA)	9.87
2004	Justin Gatlin (USA)	9.85
2008	Usain Bolt (JAM)	9.69

[1]Hayes ran a wind-assisted 9.91 in the semi-final; [2]Ben Johnson (CAN) won in 9.79 but was later disqualified

200 Metres

1900	Walter Tewksbury (USA)	22.2
1904[1]	Archie Hahn (USA)	21.6
1908	Robert Kerr (CAN)	22.6
1912	Ralph Craig (USA)	21.7
1920	Allen Woodring (USA)	22.0
1924	Jackson Scholz (USA)	21.6
1928	Percy Williams (CAN)	21.8
1932	Eddie Tolan (USA)	21.2
1936	Jesse Owens (USA)	20.7
1948	Mel Patton (USA)	21.1
1952	Andrew Stanfield (USA)	20.7
1956	Bobby Joe Morrow (USA)	20.6
1960	Livio Berruti (ITA)	20.5
1964	Henry Carr (USA)	20.3
1968	Tommie Smith (USA)	19.8
1972	Valeri Borzov (URS)	20.00
1976	Don Quarrie (JAM)	20.23
1980	Pietro Mennea (ITA)	20.19
1984	Carl Lewis (USA)	19.80
1988	Joe DeLoach (USA)	19.75
1992	Mike Marsh (USA)	20.01
1996	Michael Johnson (USA)	19.32
2000	Konstadinos Kederis (GRE)	20.09
2004	Shawn Crawford (USA)	19.79
2008	Usain Bolt (JAM)	19.79

1896, 1906 Event not held. [1]Race over straight course.

4x100 Metres Relay

1912	GBR	42.4
1920	USA	42.2
1924	USA	41.0
1928	USA	41.0
1932	USA	40.0
1936	USA	39.8
1948	USA	40.6[1]
1952	USA	40.1 (40.26)
1956	USA	39.5 (39.60)
1960	GER	39.5 (39.66)[2]
1964	USA	39.0 (39.06)
1968	USA	38.2 (38.24)
1972	USA	38.19
1976	USA	38.33
1980	Soviet Union	38.26
1984	USA	37.83
1988	Soviet Union	38.19
1992	USA	37.40
1996	Canada	37.69
2000	USA	37.61
2004	GBR	38.07
2008	JAM	37.10

1896-1908 Event not held
[1]USA originally disqualified but later reinstated; [2]USA finished first (39.60) but was disqualified

WORLD CHAMPIONS AT 100 METRES AND 200 METRES & 4x100 METRES RELAY

100 metres

1983	Carl Lewis (USA)	10.07
1987	Carl Lewis (USA)	9.93
1991	Carl Lewis (USA)	9.86
1993	Linford Christie (GBR)	9.87
1995	Donovan Bailey (CAN)	9.97
1997	Maurice Greene (USA)	9.86
1999	Maurice Greene (USA)	9.80
2001	Maurice Greene (USA)	9.82
2003	Kim Collins (SKN)	10.07
2005	Justin Gatlin (USA)	9.88
2007	Tyson Gay (USA)	9.85

2009	Usain Bolt (JAM)	9.58
2011	Yohan Blake (JAM)	9.92

200 metres

1983	Calvin Smith (USA)	20.14
1987	Calvin Smith (USA)	20.16
1991	Michael Johnson (USA)	20.01
1993	Frankie Fredericks (NAM)	19.85
1995	Michael Johnson (USA)	19.79
1997	Ato Boldon (TRI)	20.04
1999	Maurice Greene (USA)	19.80
2001	Konstantinos Kenteris (GRE)	20.04
2003	John Capel (USA)	20.30
2005	Justin Gatlin (USA)	20.04
2007	Tyson Gay (USA)	19.76
2009	Usain Bolt (JAM)	19.19
2011	Usain Bolt (JAM)	19.40

4x100 metres relay

1983	USA	37.86 WR
1987	USA	37.90
1991	USA	37.50 WR
1993	USA	37.48 (SF 37.40 EWR)
1995	CAN	38.31
1997	CAN	37.86
1999	USA	37.59
2001	RSA	38.471
2003	USA	38.06
2005	FRA	38.08
2007	USA	37.78
2009	JAM	37.31 CR
2011	JAM	37.04 WR

USA won the 2001 championship in a time of 37.96, but were disqualified after Tim Montgomery admitting to drug use in 2005.

About the author

STEVEN DOWNES has been writing on sport, and athletics, for nearly thirty years. A former editor of *Athletics Weekly* and deputy editor of *worldsport.com*, he has covered more than twenty sports at Olympic or world championship level, from netball to darts.

The co-author of the acclaimed athletics book *Running Scared*, Downes won the Royal Television Society award for sports news in 1995 and was named as Australia magazine writer of the year five years later.

Other books from SportsBooks
www.sportsbooks.ltd.uk

1908 Olympics
Keith Baker
The 1908 London Olympics can claim to be the first 'modern' sporting event which pitted nation against nation. There were rows between the British and Americans; a one-man walkover in the 400 metres when the US runners boycotted the event; a dispute over the shoes worn by one of the British tug of war teams and when the American team failed to dip their flag in front of King Edward VII it was taken as a massive snub. The best known incident came in the marathon when Italy's Dorando Pietri was disqualified for being helped over the finish line. But Queen Alexandra gave him a special gold cup. This book celebrates the first London Olympics, examines all the disputes and reveals what happened to the stars of the Games in later life. Informative and entertaining, Keith Baker's well researched book is aimed at everyone interested in sport and social history.
9781899807611
£7.99
Paperback

1948 Olympics
Bob Phillips
The 1948 Olympic Games were the first of the postwar era. Britain was still suffering the after effects of the

war. Rationing was in operation. Bomb sites remained throughout London and other major cities. Yet London took on the Games and staged them very successfully. There was no election of London as the chosen venue. The idea had first been raised in 1937 by Lord Burghley that London should hold the Games in 1944. The International Olympic Committee decided without any vote that London should have the 1948 Games.

The Games cost three quarters of a million pounds – about £77 million in today's terms. Compare that to the 2012 budget of £3.3 billion! Of course no new facilities were built. This was the make-do-and-mend Olympics. Athletes were housed in barracks and schools and were given tickets for the underground to make their own way to the stadium. Those British athletes who lived in or near London stayed at home.

9781899807543
£16.99
Hardback

Stan Greenberg's Olympic Almanack 2008
Stan Greenberg

Launched in 1984 for the Los Angeles Olympic Games, the Almanack rapidly established itself as the leading Olympic statistical book. It contains an extensive and entertaining collection of facts and figures from Athens 1896 to Athens 2004, plus the ancient Games at Olympia and the Winter Olympics. There is coverage of every summer and winter Games with detailed descriptions of venues, sports, competitors and records. There are medal tables by sport and by year which makes it the most comprehensive record of Olympic reference.

Andrew Baker of the *Daily Telegraph* said '(it) will be the first item of luggage packed by any sensible journalist or fan for their journey to Beijing next summer.'
The 2012 edition comes out in May 2012.
9781899807536
£14.99
Paperback

Conquerors of Time
Lynn McConnell

While the world suffered the great depression in the thirties, one aspect of society was booming. Track and Field had become hugely popular and milers above all. This meticulously researched book by New Zealand journalist Lynn McConnell charts the period between the LA Olympics in 1932 and the infamous Nazi Games of Berlin four years later. The main characters were New Zealander Jack Lovelock (although he was claimed by Great Britain as well). The son of immigrants Lovelock was born in New Zealand but following his studies at Oxford he returned only once to the land of his birth, preferring to remain in England. The US provided the extrovert Glenn Cunningham, the eccentric Bill Bonthron and the unlucky Gene Venzke. Then there was Italian Luigi Beccal, the 1932 Olympic 1500m champion,two British runners, Jerry Cornes and Sydney Wooderson, and Phil Edwards of Canada. Their rivalry took interest in athletics to new heights in the USA as well as fascinating the rest of the world. The four years culminated in one of the great Olympic 1500 metres final won by Lovelock in a world record.
9781899807888
£10.00
Paperback

Athletics 2011
Peter Matthews

Allyson Felix, the cover girl of Athletics 2011, focused on running more one lap races in 2010 and in winning the overall titles in the 200m and the 400m, she became the first person ever to secure top prize in two IAAF Diamond League events in the same year. She continued her dominance by winning 21 races out of 22 starts, losing only to Veronica Campbell-Brown in New York in June.

As usual the ATFS annual contains unrivalled coverage of the events of the previous year as well as chronicling the early events of 2011.

Athletics 2012 will be published in May 2012 and SportsBooks has some back issues.

9781907524028
£19.95
Paperback

All-time Greats of British Athletics
Mel Watman

Former *Athletics Weekly* editor Mel Watman, who has been writing on the sport for half a century, pays tribute to Britain's most successful athletes... from Walter George, who revolutionised miling in the 1880s to Harold Abrahams and Eric Liddell of Chariots of Fire fame, to Mary Rand, Lynn Davies and Ann Packer, to Mary Peters, Seb Coe and Steve Ovett, to Linford Christie, Sally Gunnell and Colin Jackson and Denise Lewis, Kelly Holmes and Paula Radcliffe.

The book, which runs to 242 pages plus 32 pages of photos, features in-depth profiles of 78 athletes while more than 500 appear in a British Honours List which details their main career achievements.

Seb Coe, who Watman rates as Britain's greatest ever athlete after his unique feat in retaining the Olympic 1500 metres title in Los Angeles in 1984, took time out from running Britain's preparations for the 2012 Games to write the foreword. He said: '…he has lovingly and painstakingly chronicled those individuals who have left a nation with some of the most breathtaking moments in our sporting history… I know that this book will relive those moments for everybody that reads it.'
9781899807444
£15.00
Paperback

Official History of the AAA
Mel Watman

The Amateur Athletic Association, founded in 1880 during a meeting at the Randolph Hotel in Oxford, was for many years the world's most influential governing body for track and field competition. It was the AAA which established the rules and ethos of the sport.

In this official history of the AAA, Mel Watman – who attended his first AAA Championships 60 years ago – brings to life the personalities and events which shaped athletics from its Victorian origins to the present day. Highlights of each of the prestigious AAA Championships from 1880 onwards are included in this sumptuously illustrated book.

All the great names of British athletics are featured, from the 19th century's most phenomenal runner Walter George through to more modern legends such as Dave Bedford, Seb Coe, Steve Ovett, Linford Christie and Jonathan Edwards. There is also a wealth of fascinating trivia. One of the AAA's Presidents was the judge at Dr Crippen's trial;

another climbed the Matterhorn and swam across Niagara. Competitors at the AAA Championships have included a Nobel Peace Prize winner, a best-selling novelist, a man who took part in The Great Escape of movie fame, and a leader of the Liberal Democrat party. Exhaustive lists of champions in all age groups and other compilations round off a volume which is effectively a history of British men's athletics and represents the AAA's legacy for future generations of athletes. The first official history of the AAA was written by Peter Lovesey and published in 1980.
9781907524011
£19.99
Hardback

Doping's Nemesis
Arne Ljungqvist

Prof Arne Ljungqvist (MD, PhD), who represented Sweden at high jump at the Helsinki Olympics in 1952, is one of world sports most influential administrators. He has held several of the most important posts in sport and anti-doping, including being chair of both the International Olympic Committee's and the IAAF's Medical Commissions at a time when more and more drug cheats started being caught and the sport of track and field was caught up in a maelstrom of controversy.

When the World Anti-Doping Agency was formed in in 1999 largely as a result of these problems, Ljungqvist was appointed as chair of the body's Health, Medical and Research Committee. In 2008, he was appointed as WADA's Vice President.

It was Ljungqvist who sat opposite Ben Johnson at the Seoul Olympic doping clinic in 1988 after the Canadian sprinter tested positive for drugs. The subsequent Dubin enquiry in Canada ripped open the secretive world of sports doping. Ljungqvist was also involved in the Marion Jones case when the sprinter who won five medals at the Sydney Olympics twelve years later finally admitted she had taken drugs and was stripped of her medals.

9781899807994
£17.99
Hardback

Arthur Lydiard
Garth Gilmour

Arthur Lydiard was arguably the most successful and influential running coach of the 20th century, writing some of the greatest running books.

In 1960 he burst into prominence at the Rome Olympics when two of his protégés, Peter Snell and Murray Halberg, won Olympic gold medals on the same day.

He had turned unpromising athletes into Olympic champions, and he said he could repeat the feat if only his methods, which involved building stamina and fitness through endurance running, were followed. In the next few years thousands of people heeded his word. The jogging movement was born.

But in New Zealand, Lydiard's abrasive personality upset athletics officials and he fell out of favour. New Zealand's loss became the world's gain. Lydiard's methods spread through many countries and he lectured in the United States every year up until his death at the end of 2004 as well as stocking the library of many athletes with his running books. Garth Gilmour, who was Lydiard's close friend for more than 40 years, tells for the first time the full story of the

coach's amazing career, often in Lydiard's own words. .
9781899807222
£17.99
Hardback

Passport to Football
Stuart Fuller

Stuart Fuller, author of four books of travel guides to football and a well-known blogger on football related matters, brings together his experiences on watching football in far-flung places too numerous to mention here, although they do include Moscow, Macedonia, Klagenfurt, Budapest, and Kazakhstan. Stuart brings an experienced and humorous eye to the business of watching the beautiful game, noting for example that in a game between Istanbul BBS and Rizaspor an off-side goal was allowed to stand because the linesman was arguing with the bench of the team against which he had just given a free-kick!
9781899807 83 3
£12.99
Paperback

Finn McCool's Football Club
Stephen Rea

Stephen Rea was a typical ex-pat in the US. The former Belfast journalist needed somewhere to watch and play football (or soccer as they insist on calling it over there). He found Finn McCool's Irish bar where a diverse collection of nationalities made up the regulars and the football team. They even began to get serious, joining a league. But then Hurricane Katrina struck. Rea's book is both a wry look at an obsession with football and an account of what happened to some of those who suffered one of the US's worst disasters, with an official death toll of 1,100. Many of the team and pub regulars were among those affected by the tragedy.

9781899807 86 4

£8.99

Paperback

The Victory Tests – England v Australia 1945
Mark Rowe

The five Tests between England and the Australian Services fulfilled the public appetite for sport following the end of the war in Europe. It gave the men who played in them the chance to indulge in harmless fun for once. The result was a 2-2 draw played with sportsmanship and with a sense of camaraderie missing from the modern game. Mark Rowe uncovered the full extent of legendary Australian all-rounder Keith Miller's war record – not what is has grown to be – and spoke to the surviving players in a lovingly crafted book.

9781899807 94 9

£17.99

Hardback

The Rebel Tours – Cricket's Crisis of Conscience
Peter May

The title says it all. After the d'Oliveira affair cut official ties between South Africa and England, the leading players organised tours of the Republic under the slogan that sport and politics should not mix.

The reaction of the English establishment shows in the cover. Mike Gatting, David Graveney and John Emburey face the press and although they were all banned from the international game all three were welcomed back into the establishment with a rapidity that disturbed some observers. Peter May talked to the people involved on both sides of the fence.

9781899807 80 2

£17.99

Hardback

Duckworth Lewis
Frank Duckworth & Tony Lewis

Name cricket's most famous partnership nowadays and you can forget Hobbs and Sutcliffe, Statham and Trueman or Lillee and Thomson. Instead you have to turn to Duckworth and Lewis, the two statisticians who brought order to the one-day game when rain interfered.

These days almost every weather-truncated one-day match throughout the world is decided by the Duckworth Lewis method; this book tells the story behind it; how it came into being and how the two were sometimes pilloried in the media after commentators and correspondents failed to understand the logic behind it.

Mathematicians and keen cricket fans, Frank Duckworth, editor of RSS News, the monthly magazine of the Royal Statistical Society, and Tony Lewis, retired university lecturer in mathematical subjects, grew up within a few miles of each other in West Lancashire although they didn't know one another – indeed they had planned to call their formula the 'Lancastrian' method.

The book sets out why the method was needed and gives a full explanation of how it works. Although a computer program is needed for top games, those at a lesser level can still use the tables in the book.

But the book also shows the human side of the story, how they persuaded the cricket authorities to accept their method; the mistakes they made along the way and how they corrected them; the way they developed it to take account of changes in the way the game is played, and how they coped with increasing fame. Most of all it tells how two mathematicians were able to blend their separate skills to succeed in selling a mathematical product to a non-mathematical public.

The duo became so well known that they had a racehorse named after them and then a pop group, although they have a much more famous connection with the world of music than the group The Duckworth Lewis Method: when a student at Liverpool University in the early 1960s Frank Duckworth lodged with Aunt Mimi, the woman who brought up her nephew John Lennon!

9781907524004
£12.99
Hardback

Arthur Milton
Mike Vockins

Arthur Milton was surely the last of that rare breed – a man good enough to play cricket and football for England. Twelve have had that rare distinction but the all-year-round nature of both sports makes it impossible that the feat will happen again.

Arthur had played 12 games for Arsenal when he was called up to play against Austria in 1951 because two legends, Stanley Matthews and Tom Finney, were unavailable. He decided to concentrate on cricket at the relatively young age of 29 in 1955 and Arsenal sold him to his home town club, Bristol City, for whom he made 14 appearances. He had played 84 times for Arsenal, scoring 21 times.

Usain Bolt

Although he had been picked as 12th man for the series against Australia in 1953 (and again against South Africa in 1955) he did not play his first Test until 1958. Coincidentally, he opened the innings against New Zealand at Headingley with Mike Smith, who was a double rugby and cricket England international. Milton scored 104 not out. That performance put him in the squad to visit Australia. He finished his six-Test career with 204 runs at 25.50. He was more at home playing for Gloucestershire, which he did from 1948 until 1974. He finished with more than 32,000 runs and 56 hundreds in first-class cricket. He was also outstanding in the field with 758 catches. In retirement he became a postman in Bristol and later a paper boy because he still wanted to cycle over the Downs in Bristol in the early morning. He received an honorary MA from Bristol University and could ask with a chuckle how many universities gave a degree to someone who delivered their papers!

He asked former Worcestershire secretary Mike Vockins to work on the book with him but sadly died midway through the project. Mike finished the book by speaking to many of the people who Arthur met in his long and distinguished career.

9781907524035
£18.99
Hardback